Issues in Latino Education

Race, School Culture, and the Politics of Academic Success

Mariella Espinoza-Herold

The University of Texas at El Paso

FOREWORD BY
Carlos J. Ovando

Boston ■ New York ■ San Francisco ■ Mexico City
Montreal ■ Toronto ■ London ■ Madrid ■ Munich ■ Paris
Hong Kong ■ Singapore ■ Tokyo ■ Cape Town ■ Sydney

Vice President: *Paul A. Smith*
Senior Editor: *Aurora Martínez Ramos*
Editorial Assistant: *Beth Slater*
Senior Marketing Manager: *Elizabeth Fogarty*
Editorial Production Service: *Raeia Maes*
Manufacturing Buyer: *Andrew Turso*
Cover Administrator: *Kristina Mose-Libon*
Electronic Composition: *Omegatype Typography, Inc.*

For related titles and support materials, visit our online catalogue at
www.ablongman.com.

Between the time Website information is gathered and published, some sites may
have closed. Also, the transcription of URLs can result in typographical errors. The
publisher would appreciate notification where these occur so that they may be
corrected in subsequent editions.

Library of Congress Cataloging-in-Publication Data

Data not available at the time of publication.

ISBN: 0-205-35131-X

Printed in the United States of America

10 9 8 7 6 5 4 3 2 1   07 06 05 04 03 02

CONTENTS

PREFACE

In 1984 I was sponsored by the Fulbright Foundation to undertake graduate studies in the United States. When I first arrived here from my native Peru, I recalled being greatly impressed with the quality of education in this country, the instructional facilities, free access to literature and technology, and, particularly, the wide mix of ethnically diverse college students on campus.

I rejoiced and celebrated the fact that I had chosen to be educated in the most inclusive and democratic country in this world: the United States of freedom, opportunity, and justice. This perception differed greatly from the reality of prejudice and racism against indigenous communities that I witnessed daily in my native Peru. At last, I thought I had left all that behind.

After completing a graduate degree and teaching three years at the University of Arizona, I decided it was time to explore educational issues in depth out in the real world. Hence, I obtained my first teaching position at a rural public high school and then transferred years later to large urban elementary and high school settings in southern Arizona. The reality I encountered in the public high schools did not reflect the diversity and the democratic ideals I held as a student in a university in the United States; I did not see the environment of cultural respect and educational equality that I had experienced teaching college students. Minority students in public schools were culturally and physically isolated from mainstream students, offered watered-down instruction, and had little or no say in the selection of their courses or teachers. Their cultures and identities were very often ignored, devalued, or suffocated, and their definition of success was not validated and recognized.

I remember wondering if I were living in the same country I had learned to admire while attending an American-run parochial school in South America and later as a student in college in the United States. It became clear to me in my role as a teacher that those culturally diverse students were not going to have access to the higher learning opportunities that I had had. The educational, political, and cultural barriers they faced seemed insurmountable. The diversity I observed on college campuses was mostly the faces of international college students rather than domestic minorities. I understood then why the undergraduate and graduate classes I had taught while in graduate school at the University of Arizona were mostly filled with white students and hardly any Latino students.

At this point I began to explore the real meaning of the word *democracy* and this country's founding principles. I set out to explore the reasons for these deep societal inequities all too evident in public institutions. I became further stimulated after taking graduate classes from Professors Richard Ruiz and Terry McCarty at the University of Arizona and after reading Jim Cummins' powerful research on minority language issues in Toronto. I have always believed that education is the most valuable investment you can make for yourself. Education opens doors, but, most important, it is essential for human progress and the welfare of our planet. My parents were deeply committed to my education and always encouraged me to persevere to attain my educational goals. Growing up in my native Peru, I remember few gifts, but there was always an exciting book I would share with my siblings. After I graduated from an institution in the United States and began teaching in public schools, I made many painful discoveries particularly about colleagues and school administrators who brought elitist attitudes to classrooms and who defended the status quo. It was not uncommon for me to hear teachers talk about the "cultural inferiority" of Latinos that placed doubts on their academic ability or questioned the communities' value on education.

Essentially, these teachers believed that the Latino families' lack of education was responsible for the students' dropping out of school. Not only do all these explanations blame the victims for their own failures, but they also seem to be self-serving because these same educators benefit from the status quo in public education.

I did not intentionally choose to write about these issues. The subject of this text came to me and evolved from my twelve-year work as an educator with high school-age Latino adolescents. From them, I learned of their individual and collective struggles to achieve educational equity while trying to preserve their cultural identities. The intent of this book is to examine—mainly through the voices and views of Latino students themselves—the factors contributing to the differential school success among certain nonmainstream students in southern Arizona public high schools.

Acknowledgments

This book has grown over several years out of many contexts. First, it developed from my doctoral thesis, and I owe profound gratitude to members of my committee who were most helpful and supportive of this project. I would like to express my thanks and deepest appreciation to Roseann Gonzalez for her encouragement, her insightful ideas, and her reading of the manuscript. Her intelligence and scholarly work are a continuous source of inspiration and a credit to the Mexican-American academic community. I also owe a debt of thanks to my mentor, Terry McCarty, whom I admire for her impressive professionalism and genuine concern for the issues of lesser-privileged populations. Terry and the rest of my dissertation committee, Richard Ruiz, Luis Moll, and Arminda Fuentevilla, gave useful criticisms of an earlier version of the book and encouraged me to have it published. Denis Viri has been (and will continue to be) family, friend, and colleague. His intellectual questioning and our fruitful discussions gave shape to this book during the early days when it was only an idea. I especially want to thank him for his comradeship and moral support in those days when I struggled with school bureaucracies while advocating for Latino children in schools. I am also grateful to Carlos Ovando and Jim Cummins, whose work and scholarship I admire. It has meant a lot for me to have their respected voices here as well. Many thanks go to Raeia Maes for the meticulous and professional editing and to Aurora Martínez Ramos, acquisitions editor for Allyn and Bacon/Longman. I thank her for her vote of confidence and assistance with this project.

In addition, my work has been greatly supported from the distance by my parents Carlos and Mercedes, and by my friends in Europe, Robert Baer and Christiane Delozanne. I thank them for their faith in my ability to write this book in a language I did not grow up with. I thank my daughter, Jean Andrea, who shared the testing times of graduate work and later book-writing. In this sense, she is the coauthor of this book. Her patience and encouragement were truly a labor of love. I gratefully acknowledge the reviewers: Wendy Brandon, Rollins College; Matthew B. Dwyer, Teachers College, Columbia University; Craig A. Hughes, Central Washington University; Linda Medearis, Texas A&M International University; John Petrovic, University of Alabama; and Buenaventura Torres-Ayala, University of Texas at San Antonio, and thank them for their helpful suggestions. Finally, I want to acknowledge Carla, Manny, and the many hundred bright Latino high school students in Arizona for putting up with my intrusions into their lives and for giving me their time and thought in the interviews. Many of them wondered skeptically if their voices were ever going to be heard. To them, I dedicate this work.

FOREWORD

No social entity as complex as a school can function without considerable trust. Trust is most effective when it is taken for granted. But when students of color with legitimate social differences from White students are brought into a school under a colorblind perspective that will not acknowledge such differences, trouble is bound to arise. Negative stereotypes held by many White educators and simple unfamiliarity with the social patterns of students of color and their communities compound these difficulties. One important kind of trouble on the part of White adults is a fear of raising racial issues, a fear that silences what could become a healthy, if sometimes painful, racial dialogue.

> —Mary Haywood Metz, Foreword to *The Color of Bureaucracy: The Politics of Equity in Multicultural School Communities* (Wadsworth, 2001)

At the dawn of the new millennium, most of us are no longer surprised to learn that the United States is becoming even more racially, culturally, and linguistically diverse—a browner, more multilingual, and globally linked society. These population changes, the *demographic imperative,* have consequently produced large numbers of students whose first language is not English. Yet, unfortunately, most school administrators and teachers tend not to be well prepared to meet such students' cultural, linguistic, emotional, and cognitive needs.

Many mainstream educators, who incidentally may themselves be members of stigmatized racial and ethnolinguistic groups who have bought into an assimilationist ideology, believe that in order to be successful in the United States, English language learners must relinquish their ancestral languages and cultures in favor of English-only schooling. These teachers and administrators thereby invoke the colorblind ideology, which intentionally blurs or erases racial, ethnic, gender, class, or linguistic variables in their students' lives. On one hand, as Sonia Nieto observes in her book, *Affirming Diversity,* colorblindness may seem to be pro social justice and *nondiscriminatory*—"I don't see Black or White," a teacher will say, "I see only students." On the other hand, as Nieto also points out, ". . . color blindness may result in *refusing to accept differences* and therefore accepting the dominant culture as the norm. It may result in denying the very identity of our students, thereby making them invisible." Not surprisingly, even though these educators' intentions are good, their failure to acknowledge students' differing cultural and linguistic identities too often creates resentment, resulting in a lack of trust and academic disengagement that often lead to high dropout rates, especially among Latino high school students.

In *Issues in Latino Education*, Mariella Espinoza-Herold courageously and insightfully examines what it means to know and to trust Latino students, and to care about their futures, within the cultural, programmatic, biographical, and political context of a southwestern high school with a large Latino representation. Like Angela Valenzuela's notion of "care" in *Subtractive Schooling: U.S.–Mexican Youth and the Politics of Caring*, Espinoza-Herold situates "care" in a structural and historical perspective and suggests that in order to create successful schooling practices with Latino students, school administrators must affirm the lived experiences of both voluntary and involuntary immigrants—their ancestral cultures, their social contexts, and their prior schooling experience. Anchored in these past contexts, schools can then provide teaching and learning environments that maximize and take advantage of the plurality of experiences to create exciting teaching and learning challenges and opportunities for *all* students, not just those who speak standard English and come from middle- and upper-class backgrounds.

As we navigate the turbulent societal and educational waters of the new millennium, Espinoza-Herold's book affirms Mary Haywood Metz's words: "that to say one is colorblind, in hopes of being fair, is in fact to say one is blind, unwillingly to fully recognize the students and parents with whom one actually deals." The book also serves as a harbinger of challenges and opportunities to create a better society in the United States that will be increasingly intertwined with the global village.

Carlos J. Ovando
Arizona State University

Introduction

Genesis of This Work: The Rural Scenario

My intellectual interest in the success and failure of schools and in the high school dropout phenomenon—highly visible in Arizona schools—began during my first year as a public school teacher in a rural school in southern Arizona. At that time, I had just finished a Master's degree in Linguistics and English as a Second Language. I was highly energized and focused on putting into actual practice those theories of second language acquisition and bilingualism I had spent several years learning about. It was hard for me to imagine then that this first experience in a public school classroom in 1989 was going to provoke a dramatic shift in my intellectual interests from linguistic theory to a passionate advocacy for social justice issues and human rights. It never became clearer to me, after that first experience 12 years ago, that the interactions between students and teachers are far more essential for students' school success than the best language methodologies, brilliant lecturers, or innovative language research employed in the classroom. As Jim Cummins (1996) stated in his influential framework, "coercive vs. collaborative relations of power," and later verified by the high school students with whom my research involved, educators define their roles, behavior, assumptions, and expectations interactively when they come into contact with students from culturally diverse backgrounds. If the interaction is of a positive nature, some students will initiate a process of self-empowerment and self-affirmation of their identities. This directly contributes to their ability to persevere academically, overcome obstacles, and achieve their educational aspirations. Negative interactions, however, destroy their self-esteem, make them feel devalued and inferior, distort their identity, and ultimately push them out of the system.

Over a decade ago, as I began that first journey inside a rural American public high school, I had assumed my employer wanted to utilize my freshly gained knowledge in English as a Second Language and Linguistics to implement a program for the growing number of Mexican immigrant students enrolled at the school that year. Later, I realized that the administration was far more interested in making use of my French credentials to offer a new

French program and relegate my ESL assignment to a secondary function. Thus, while the school authorities invested large amounts of money in textbooks, technology, and materials to carry out a full-blown French program, the Arizona mainstream teachers at this school were desperately complaining about crowded classrooms now filled with "strange" students they did not know how to teach. The enormous frustrations these educators faced logically gave way to intense animosity and anger toward this new group of students who were perceived as a burden because of their English language limitations and overall academic inferiority. Similar to Deyhle's (1995) research findings of Navajo students, which confirms the "deficit hypothesis" common in American schools, the bicultural students in this school were judged by what they *didn't* have (English language, middle-class EuroAmerican values, money) rather than strengths they brought with them in the form of community, strong family values, Spanish language ability, and religious beliefs.

During the three years I remained at the school, dozens of bright students dropped out and violent interracial conflicts among students escalated. Daily, the school's minority students either crowded detention rooms, were suspended, or received failing grades in ratios far exceeding those of their Anglo counterparts. Some of these students managed to develop a toughness that allowed them to stay in school in spite of their perception that some educators and administrators did not like them. Those resilient enough to stay in school were forced to accept a form of inner exile in which they were continually discouraged in their attempts to succeed despite rigid policies and practices and, in some cases, direct remarks from teachers and administrators. In my interaction with faculty members, I soon learned that bilingual education was a bad word in this closed conservative educational community that was financed largely with the property taxes of wealthy retirees. With the aid of a few concerned and caring mainstream educators who felt education was not just a "job" but a true mission, we managed to design a "nonlabeled" pilot program. This program offered science, math, and American government classes in the Spanish language in the mornings. An introduction to content key words in English was also offered. The same lesson was offered to the students in the afternoon in English by a group of mainstream teachers who voluntarily agreed to assist these students by adjusting their teaching styles and methods. At the end of the first year, we started seeing great improvements not only in the steady decrease of dropouts but also in the academic improvement of these students. An encounter with one of these students several years later greatly contributed to the conceptualization of the ideas behind the writing of this book. Today she is well on her way to becoming a secondary bilingual educator.

As the rapid and unexpected gains obtained through this minipilot program began to gain visibility in terms of the empowerment of these minority students at the school, there were signs that the powers that be were feeling threatened. Motivation among these students rose to the point that 20% of the Mexican-American students began to outperform their mainstream counterparts in core curriculum classes such as mathematics and social studies. Upon learning about this opportunity, students from neighboring districts transferred into our school at various times during the academic year. Thus, the task of educating greater numbers of students in both languages became a real challenge, given that we had only one bilingual teacher for the project. The small and supportive group of educators who strongly believed in this "closeted" form of bilingual education soon presented a petition to the school district administration to hire additional bilingual personnel for its increasingly diverse population. The request was denied and an English as a Second Language program designed for immediate transition into English language instruction was instituted in its place. This denial was anticipated by some of the educators who, along with me, drafted the request. They all knew that the word *bilingual* carried a very negative stigma in this rural and very conservative Arizona school district.

Genesis of This Work: The Urban Reality

After my experience teaching at a rural school district, I later accepted a teaching position in an urban public high school in one of the largest school districts in Arizona. During my transition from a small rural school into a secondary school with a student population exceeding 2,500, I experienced some unexpected as well as anticipated differences. Present-day secondary schools are usually very large bureaucracies. Decision-making policies, curriculum materials, and even innovative activities that educators try to implement are often controlled by external requirements beyond the direct influence of the school and its teachers.

Latinos and other ethnically diverse students are concentrated in many large urban schools. Therefore, services and programs to accommodate their needs are more evident and the processes of delivering these services are much slower, less personal, and bureaucratic. The testimonies of the students in this book reveal that the frustrations Latino students experience in schools are due to the lengthy and inefficient processes utilized in schools to resolve problems. During my first months as an educator in this crowded urban school, it became more evident to me that secondary teachers were more knowledgeable of current research in their fields in contrast to their counterparts in an isolated rural setting. Obviously, this had something to do with the geographical proximity to higher learning institutions. The human relations and interactions between students and teachers palpably mirrored those that exist in the larger society. Class distinctions, as well as the national political pendulum that drive the school's policies and programs, are more evident in urban school student common areas and classrooms. I perceived that unequal economic and social conditions that are present in low-income culturally diverse communities in inner cities are replicated educationally in urban schools.

Coming from a rural public school into a large urban institution in which minority groups were the majority high school population, I knew I was going to encounter a few more incongruities in the schooling dynamics. Added to the fact that the faculty and administrators were of diverse ethnic origins, I was encouraged by a philosophy that promoted multiculturalism and that spoke of teachers as change agents. But after a few months teaching in these big "orbes," I found that behind this picture of social activism and presumed democracy there were hierarchies, stressed and discriminated students, silenced minority faculty (nonmainstream educators who were afraid to advocate for bicultural students and place their jobs at risk), and programs driven by state education mandates. I started asking questions: Why is lesson planning a rigid zero-tolerance discipline program? Why are daily grades seen and taught as the focus and essence of curriculum and instruction? Shouldn't we be helping students ask what is worthwhile to know and experience? Speaking out only brought reprisals and being summoned to one-on-one meetings with school administrators. Needless to say, my ideas supporting an inclusive curriculum were not well received and resulted in several unsuccessful attempts to not renew my teaching contract and to push me out of the school. Most minority teachers knew that in order to preserve their jobs it was safer to leave things as they were or "buy" into the district's politics of publicizing a humanistic rhetoric but implementing only minor superficial changes in the schools.

During this second experience as a public school teacher in the United States, I was given again a dual teaching assignment in this southside barrio school in which students of Mexican origin comprised 65% of the total school population. Again I was faced with the contrastive dilemma of teaching French as an academically prestigious language while also teaching Spanish, which was considerably undervalued because of its association with the Mexican and border Spanish-speaking communities that surrounded the school. It was the first time I encountered large numbers of Latinos who, being former native speakers of the language, were victims of this linguistic devaluation. I learned that parents of many of my students had purposely chosen not to teach their children Spanish, believing that the children would achieve greater economic and social status by speaking English only. Ironically, many of these students, as part of their adolescent awakening, were searching for their roots and enthusiastically enrolled in formal Spanish classes as a way to regain their Latino identity.

At a professional development workshop I gave a presentation on using writing as a method to motivate students to increase their basic skills and critical creative thinking processes. My expertise teaching diverse students was well received by some colleagues. I gained professional respect in the school and some caring colleagues acted as mediators with the school administration. In my ESL, Spanish, or French classes writing critically was a tool my students and I greatly enjoyed.

I entered their work in a national essay contest in which they needed to explicate the importance of bilingualism. The students were especially enthusiastic about this assignment and some even interviewed their parents and relatives to determine the real reasons behind linguistic and culture discontinuity that came to exist across generations in their families and communities. After many revisions and several weeks of hard and determined work, we submitted candidly written essays that recounted the punishments, rejection, and pain their parents and families experienced for speaking Spanish in schools in the 1950s and 1960s. As I read their essays, I reflected on Jim Cummins' (1996) observations that overt or covert negative messages were being sent to the minority student: "To be accepted within the mainstream society students had to become invisible and inaudible; culture and language should be left at home" (p. 2). I was soon to learn through following events that this reflection is as applicable today as it ever was.

The practice of exploring their cultural identity and re-evaluating their ancestral culture and language through the essays turned out to be a very empowering experience for this group of adolescents. They also became extremely motivated to relearn their language because it was associated with their cultural roots. A few weeks later, the new school principal, an African American female, informed us that she had received a call from the organization that sponsored the essay contest announcing that two students from my Spanish class had been awarded first and second place for the state. She also said that she had refused to allow the monetary and travel awards to be presented to my students because she felt that they were not placed in bilingual classes but were students studying Spanish as a foreign language. In her view, this disqualified them from the contest. Never in my career had I observed a more crestfallen group of students.

Mexican-American high school students struggling for a new identity (as the ones in the Spanish class described above) usually collectively develop ambivalent views about themselves as a result of disempowering school experiences. At the same time, they debate over the appropriate course of action needed to succeed in life. In critical theory, the school episode exposed above represents the "hegemony of violence" alluded to by Macedo and Bartolome (1998) in which school climates that promote xenophobic and prejudicial feelings against certain cultures kill any hope for empowerment and success among the oppressed.

The critical incident narrated above further heightened my awareness of the processes and events that critically disempower students of nonmainstream communities. The reasons for the high dropout rates, low performance, and lack of success of many bicultural students were becoming abundantly clear to me. My experience of this incident, and many others that followed, is the driving force behind this critical ethnography. While interacting with students during these incidents, I was continually startled by the insights they would provide about their own experiences. Therefore, I decided to expose some of the school dynamics that empower or disempower students in schools through their own words and experiences. *Issues in Latino Education* delivers a forum in which students and educators are allowed to define and provide material insights into the power structures that control a school's success.

Educators: Where Do We Stand?

As an educator, I have varied and mixed emotions about the future of education in the United States in our new millennium. The political and social orientation of this country is often polarized and at odds with itself. Democratic ideals often prevail only to be later overcome in practice by provincialism and Anglo ethnocentrism of a few powerful individuals who control the community's educational dreams. Such incongruities directly affect those culturally diverse communities that have for years attempted to come to terms with poverty, educational disadvantage, and lack of opportunities. American social ambivalence is manifested in such incongruities as racial and ethnic discrimination contrasted with the insistence that equal opportunity exists. Incongruities are apparent when the government claims that diverse populations are included and their cultures respected while at the same time affirmative action, bilingual education, and other key protective programs that guarantee the rights of minorities are being dismantled across the country.

These incongruities are also perceived in larger spheres. On a global level, there is increased economic interdependence and international collaboration in a variety of areas, especially in Europe and Asia. These are acknowledged in the United States but not without frequent retreats into American isolationism and cultural hegemony. In a campaign speech George W. Bush praised President Vicente Fox of Mexico and spoke enthusiastically about the need to develop closer economic ties and trade relations with our southern neighbor. In that same speech Bush also turned vitriolic, emphasizing America's need to protect and further militarize against intruders at its southern border. As we know, our government's anti-immigrant feelings have increased as a result of the tragic events of September 11. Our airports, harbors, and borders are zealously guarded, and all immigrants, regardless of their status, are perceived as potential terrorists.

On the education front, educators in the United States constantly belabor the need for students to acquire international languages in order to compete more adequately in the world marketplace. But now 23 states have enacted English-only laws and two states with the largest Latino populations (Arizona and California) have practically outlawed bilingual education.

Incongruities between what is written and what is actually implemented, along with a lack of a clear direction in our nation's educational goals, seem to be the rule at the beginning of the twenty-first century. They are reflected in the educational outcomes of nonmainstream students across the country who have not shown significant improvement. However, there are those rare occasions when our educational authorities and some progressive politicians clearly spell out their educational visions and objectives.

While attending the Salzburg Seminar, in which educators from all corners of the world gathered to discuss the future of public education, I had the opportunity to interact with the then First Lady Hillary Clinton who was visiting Europe at the time. I asked her opinion on the successful Swiss educational system that integrates four official languages into the school curriculum. I shared with her that in recent legislature the Swiss government had invested a considerable amount of money to revitalize the Romanche language (spoken by 1% of the Swiss population) as well as to implement innovative bilingual programs in Canton Chur. She became defensive at my question, replying that the United States would never become Switzerland. Hearing her answer, I was struck by the ideological homogeneity of both the Republican and Democratic parties on issues of recognizing, officializing, or at least truly incorporating languages other than English into schools in the United States, given the increasing international economic interdependence. The possibility of a true "ethnolinguistic democracy" (Fishman, 1995), the equal status and linguistic respect for languages other than English in the United States, is an issue often received with tension and conflict by the dominant majority in this country. It is obvious that it will remain only a dream in the face of a fierce enforcement of the English language hegemony.

Ron Unz, the quintessential advocate for the dismantling of bilingual education in California and Arizona has now as his third target the state of New York. According to Unz (2000), 150,000 immigrant kids remain "imprisoned in bilingual education" there. He further claims that the shift to English immersion has the support of the press and the general population, many of whom are one or two generations removed from the old country.

Unz, a software developer and a California millionaire, has made full restoration of melting pot ideology his goal. Unfortunately, his words resonate with the thinking of many professional educators, some of whom are represented in his work. Worse yet, many of these educators would not publicly admit to what Unz (2000) professes openly:

> Similarly, public school curricula which glorify obscure ethnic figures at the expense of the giants of American history have no place in the melting pot framework. Multiculturalist ideology, which claims that Asian students can only identify with Asian heroes, Black students only with Black heroes, and so forth, is not only demeaning and divisive, it is also false . . . families must remain free to preserve as much—or as little—of their traditional ethnic heritage as they desire, but our public schools should provide a single, unifying American culture rather than encouraging ethnic fragmentation. (p. 4)

His words contrast greatly with the statements of the students in this study. According to the students, the lack of interest in school has to do with the lack of connection between the school curriculum and the reality of their communities and their experiences. The apathy and academic disengagement many of them experienced had to do with contradictory views of success between mainstream teachers and Latino youth. Subsequent chapters of this book relate that when students were in classes that addressed the historical contributions of diverse communities to the development of this nation, they viewed themselves as being represented within their schools. They felt their historical contributions validated their culture and language. Those few empowering classes become the sole reason that some were able to persevere academically.

The same rings true for bicultural students regarding bilingual education and curricula. In spite of (a) overwhelming evidence of the psycho-educational benefits of bilingual education explained by Cummins (1989, 1996), (b) the ample academic gains highlighted in long-term national studies (Collier, 1992; Ramirez, Yuen, & Ramey, 1991), and (c) the great success of numerous dual-language and gradual-exit programs across the country (Krashen, 1998, 1999), little is being done to equip more bilingual programs with much needed bilingual books in school libraries across the country. The book shortage and the limited training bilingual educators receive (especially concerns related to higher literacy levels and academic writing in the nonmainstream tongue) prevent bilingual programs from obtaining better educational outcomes and from demonstrating their solid cognitive benefits.

Bilingual education in the United States has been successfully utilized by conservative and racist political groups as an anti-immigrant weapon and as a way to instill fear among the White population of a growing Mexican cultural and linguistic invasion. The rationale behind the passing of Proposition 227 in California and Proposition 203 in Arizona has been well documented by Crawford (2000) and Gonzalez and Melis (2000). If advocates of bilingual education truly wanted support, they should have promoted the benefits of bilingualism as a legitimate social policy that can be applied on behalf of all Americans rather than focusing on it as a transitional deficit-reducing educational strategy for immigrants and minorities. Crawford (2000) argues that bilingual education must be depoliticized so that it can be viewed more rationally as a worthy community-based pedagogy and as a benefit to all of our society.

On the political front, the recently appointed George W. Bush multi-ethnic presidential cabinet was orchestrated to convince us of ethnic inclusion. It was an attempt to overshadow the ethnic confrontations and frictions resulting from the recent election of an African American backed mayor in predominantly Hispanic Los Angeles. The students in this study eloquently narrate similar ethnic confrontations and frictions in large urban secondary schools, illuminating McLaren's (1998) position that

In the United States we are living a time of undeclared war. Each day we negotiate our way through mine sown terrains of confrontation and uncertainty surrounding the meaning and purpose of identity. (p. 411)

On the educational front, decades of cosmetic educational reforms and billions of dollars spent continue to produce skin color predictors of standardized test scores and appalling high dropout rates, which in many states as in Arizona remain unchanged. Furthermore, there are some states such as Texas, in which high school attrition rates have drastically worsened (Valenzuela, 1999), and in which thousands of future promising Latino teachers are abandoning their educational aspirations. The "accountability fever" has driven the state of Texas to impose a rigid standardized Examination for Certification of Educators in Texas (ExCET) as a requirement for state certification. Logically, the underfunded higher learning institutions that serve a student body of 90% Latinos are the ones most affected by these mandates. This is a byproduct of the nation's schizophrenia about diversity. Before the United States can become a true working partner with the rest of the world, it must come to terms with its hegemonic responses to its own people and diversity.

The students interviewed in *Issues in Latino Education* support the finding that some mainstream educators continue to pathologize and "blame the victim" where multicultural students are concerned. Although needed now more than ever before, educators who are willing to challenge the broader power structures and nurture alliances and collaborative interactions with academically disadvantaged students seem to be the exception rather than the rule.

In lieu of the recently passed (politically charged) antibilingual education laws in the state of Arizona that are part of the anti-immigrant mind set, it is not surprising that few educators dare to challenge the broader power structures for fear of risking their jobs. Following the critical incidents I mentioned above, I set out to observe more closely classrooms and educators of bicultural students at the high school level. As I began my doctoral studies, I requested the school district grant me a half-time leave of absence that would allow me to maintain contact with students while pursuing my educational aspirations. Thus, rather than a formal teaching assignment, I shared the responsibility of supervising a new program that would provide tutoring, academic assistance, and supervision to incoming freshman high school students. This resulted in one of the most enriching and productive experiences in my 21 years as an educator.

The daily one-on-one interaction with students of all ethnic backgrounds in a school of over 2,500 students gave me the opportunity to learn about their fears and frustrations, their inner world and identity, their perspectives of what constituted good teaching and good teachers, and the environment they found as the most productive to succeed academically. There were a number of additional critical incidents during that year in which I felt compelled to be an advocate for the rights of minority students. Incidents between certain teachers and their students of color clearly reflected the negative views that some educators bring to classrooms. I considered it my task to listen to the claims of bicultural students and expose educators who continuously stigmatized, harassed, and isolated young African Americans and other minority students in the classroom. I saw it my responsibility to invite counselors to get out of their comfortable offices in those mini-cities called high schools and reach out to more students. Many nonmainstream students ignored the right they had to enroll in classes of their choice or were unaware of the meaning of a grade point average, its importance, or the way to calculate it. I considered my task to encourage dozens of Mexican-descent students who felt offended and humiliated by a librarian, who openly displayed his favoritism for mainstream students in the distribution of books or the use of computers in the library, to write letters of complaint to the school administrator. I agreed with the students when I signed their petition requesting that the school administration not dismantle the bilingual classes. As was expected, my protection of ethnically diverse and disempowered students took me on more than one occasion to seek protection from the teaching union. The union's perception of my "insubordination" and "violation of district policies" put my job in danger. Fortunately, my excellent teaching practices, classroom evaluations, and the support of students and their families played a decisive role in the outcome of school hearings and accusations.

The price for advocating the cause of ethnically diverse students is at times a high one to pay, but the satisfaction you get is incomparable, when as a result of your interventions, new practices are employed and bicultural students acquire a sense of self-empowerment.

In spite of my early conditioning in my country of origin, it is no longer surprising to me that Latinos today experience the greatest school attrition and low postsecondary enrollment rates in the United States. At the same time, ongoing legislation doles out vast amounts of federal and state funding and implements multiple intervention programs.

Yet, like the students in this study, there are some strong spirited, resourceful adolescents who do manage to succeed. They resist conforming to a system that undermines their cultural identity, excludes them from meaningful participation in school, and eventually forces them out.

It is not the intention of this book to presuppose that teachers and school administrators are the scoundrels in the failure of low-income urban students of color. Many of today's educators (as the testimonies of teachers will reveal in this study) are the products of communities that endured a history of racism and exclusion. However, as the maxim suggests, many of them teach the way they learned, replicating much of their own earlier experiences. My intent is not to point a finger but to expose the pervasiveness of cultural predispositions that condition society in the United States to interpret student failure as individual failure, therefore ignoring the systemic forces that are connected with school injustices. This critical ethnography will also explore the sense of frustration and powerlessness felt by the teachers of students of color in schools. Schools do not exist in isolation. They are part of a larger community and respond to the decisions made by people who are often disconnected from classrooms. These decisions deeply affect programs and classroom dynamics that have considerable impact on students with the greatest economic and educational need.

This critical ethnography constitutes an exploration into the development of a Latino identity that is forced into the shadows of an already adverse environment. It is a testimony to young adolescents who are aware of a prejudiced world around them and who are committed to eliminate a racism that virtually causes their underachievement and failure. Their statements tell us that ethnically diverse adolescents learned through contextual information gathered in various interactions between teachers and students that their economic status, and the image that the dominant society has of their culture and language, should not destroy their ethnic identity, their dreams for a better life and their self-confidence. At a time when the "Hispanophobia" to which Crawford alludes (2000) increases in parts of the United States—when we are flooded by negative media messages portraying immigrants caught at the border and treated as delinquents for the sole crime of looking for a job— the Mexican-descent students in this book who resisted against the devaluing of their culture provide testimony to what they can become when they encounter caring educators, empowering classes, and a meaningful school curriculum.

Finally, this book is grounded in genuine research in schools serving culturally distinct students. It invites educators, school administrators, and policy makers to continue re-examining cultural hegemony in schools through listening to the voices of bicultural students themselves. Students who are struggling to find strength in their condition of being "different," who want to fully participate in the events of the world, and who want to be heard need a supportive and liberating educational experience.

The text is organized into seven chapters. Chapter 1 provides a brief theoretical framework for the study and it reviews the literature on differential group success and failure. Chapter 2 offers an analysis of the historical educational exclusion of Latinos and it includes current statistical information on the reality of Latinos in Arizona and across the nation. At the same time, it gives an overview of recent successful programs that are producing some positive changes for some populations of color. It also describes the urban school district, demographic data, and its social climate prior to and during 1994–1997 when this study took place. Chapters 3 and 4 detail the individual case studies of two students of Latino origin, their life accounts and individual interpretation of their schooling experiences, and their views of personal success. The students' narratives are charged with deep analysis of the complexities of staying in school versus leaving school and on their views on how institutions frame Latino students' identities and aspirations. Chapter 5 enters into the worlds of 33 urban high school teachers who define their role as educators of students of color and their views about Latinos in schools and high school success. Through surveys and interviews they share their interpretations of the problems of Latino students' underachievement and dropping out. The chapter also offers a critical and often overlooked examination of the differences and similarities between educator and student views. Chapter 6 also braids the case study findings and the teachers' viewpoints with critical educational theory. Chapter 7 includes the students' recommendations for educational reform suggesting a call for greater activism and deeper probing of unhealthy social pathologies in education. The chapter also explores the implications and deeper meaning of these interactions and suggests a plan of action for teachers, administrators, and education policy makers.

1 Conceptual Underpinnings of Latino School Success and Failure

Why is ethnic background such a potent predictor of academic success? Finding an answer to this question has been the focus of ongoing, passionate debates in the academic and public arenas for several decades. School learning and achievement of nonmainstream students are influenced by persistent and complex socioeconomic, cultural, historical, political, and ideological forces. There are no complete answers to this problem and the interaction of many interrelated factors forces additional microethnographic testing of theoretical frameworks in urban schools and classrooms in the United States. The information found through the testimonies of students and teachers in this book is viewed and explained by various disciplines and theoretical underpinnings. These interconnected theoretical interpretations, which have informed our understanding of the phenomenon of school success and failure among Mexican origin populations, do not form a conceptual framework in the conventional sense; they are a coalition of concepts that worked together as a strategy for this research.

Research Perspectives on Underachievement of Bicultural Students and *The Politics of Success*

The phenomenon of school underachievement among Latino and other nonmainstream students has been well documented (Davidson, 1996; Fine, 1991; Nieto, 1992; Romo & Falbo, 1996; Valenzuela, 1999). These researchers examined Ogbu's (1978) influential macro-enthnographic study in which he explained this phenomenon by focusing on the economic effects of societal structures. He took into account the responses of oppressed populations to these societal structures. For Ogbu (1995), the problem of why different groups of nonmainstream students succeed while others fail is answered within the tradition of the class analysis argument and, in particular, from the economic-reproductive perspective. He looked at differences among minority groups, in terms of birthplace, length of residence in the host country, socio-historic constraints, and their influence on academic achievement. Ogbu's theories provided great insights into understanding Latino students' underachievement. In particular, his typology of immigrant versus domestic minorities has greatly influenced this study. However, it left me with many questions, especially on the lack of connection of his theory to classroom realities and on the rigorous nature of the explanation. Ogbu (1995) claimed that the importance that immigrant students confer on school learning is superior to that of caste-like domestic minorities and their communities. He argued that the nature of the relationship between the nonmainstream culture and the dominant culture is different for each different minority group. It is obvious that Ogbu's theoretical base lies in the emphasis on differences among minority groups mainly as a result of socio-historical and societal economic-reproductive effects.

My observations of Latino students, however, both immigrant and American born, suggest a host of more subtle factors at work that are not explained by Ogbu's (1995) fixed dualism of voluntary immigrant and involuntary American born minority students. My hypothesis is that the nature of the relationship between both groups and the mainstream culture presents more similarities than differences. The concerns of both Latino student groups, immigrant and American born, were perceived in the same manner by most members of the dominant group. As a practitioner in the field, I have observed more commonalities than differences, both among minority groups and within groups, in terms of their relationships with the school system, including teachers. Nevertheless, both groups continue to perform poorly in schools in the United States, in comparison with mainstream students, mainly as a result of their low social status within the dominant society.

Many researchers (Cummins, 2000; Davidson, 1996; Foley, 1991; Mehan, Hubbard, & Villanueva, 1994; Valdes, 1996) have also found that Ogbu's dichotomy fails to explain intragroup variance among minority groups. In the case of Latinos and Mexican origin populations in the United States, as the federal statistics presented in Chapter 2 verify, in recent years the Latino immigrant group failed and dropped out of school in larger numbers than Latinos born in the United States.

In addition to the complexities of intragroup variability, there are some researchers (Durand & Massey, 1992; Valdes, 1996) who believe that Mexican-descent students do not fit into either of Ogbu's two fixed groups of minorities. According to Valdes (1996), the Mexican-American community includes populations who have been native here for generations and who see themselves as the indigenous original settlers of parts of the United States. Additionally, there are also Mexican origin individuals who have arrived later as either legal or illegal immigrants but have lived here for several generations. Thus, generalizations about Mexican-American individuals, their status, and their views on colonization and its impact on the educational success or failure of their children are difficult to make. Valdes related, "Dual typologies are hard to construct because there are simultaneous categories, both immigrant-minorities and caste-minorities, within this single population" (p. 25).

When talking about immigrant groups, we see many distinctions, such as social status, reasons for migration, age at time of migration, and the circumstances and available resources upon arrival. These factors affect the composition of the migration and at the same time shape the immigrant student's achievement in school. Thus, it is almost impossible to make generalizations about populations in continuous movement across the border and between two worlds. The complexities of dominant-subordinated group relationships and intragroup variance are difficult to explain in a single fixed typology.

From a plain theoretical perspective, the understanding of the difficulties surrounding the education of nonmainstream children must include, as Persell (cited in Valdes, 1996) has argued, the integration of four levels of analysis: societal, institutional, interpersonal, and interpsychic. A sound theory of educational inequality, he argued, must take into account the division of power within a particular society and the ideology behind that division. It must consider factors such as the knowledge, skills, attitudes, and ideologies that teachers, administrators, and counselors bring to schools and classrooms. It must also consider individual students' qualities and backgrounds as well as the school's instruction and its context.

Latino students, immigrant or American born (voluntary or involuntary), enter our public schools with high aspirations and the desire to pursue the "American dream." When they affirm their own definition of educational success and their own views of the "American dream," their voices are often dismissed and ignored. Frequently, teachers' attitudes, beliefs, practices, and their own culturally mediated interpretation of success affect the access to academic achievement of the very same students they are trying to serve.

This book guides us through such a world—a world in which Latino students are confronted with a dual and contradictory interpretation of educational success, a school world, I argue, in which students are forced to choose between two conceptions of educational attainment. One conception affirms and embraces success through the acceptance of the students' life experiences, points of view, and their own culturally driven definitions of success. The other conception sees success in a reductionist and assimilationist way, one that promotes the erosion of Latino students' values and forms of knowledge and one that restricts forms of success to those valued and dictated by the dominant culture. Thus, the common claim that some minorities do better than others, given the same cultural and linguistic constraints, needs to be examined more closely in the context of teacher–student interactions, cultural incongruities, power relations, and other school-based, subtle micro-variables that are often overlooked.

Cummins (1997, 2000) through his influential work drew our attention to the role of teachers and schools in promoting and exacerbating the disparities among nonmainstream and mainstream students. Cummins' distinction of coercive and collaborative relations of power seems to have provided the most effective explanation of the issues of differential school success among nonmainstream students. As he explained, coercive relations of power refer to the control that a dominant group exercises over a subordinated nation, group, or individual. This control is often manifested in discourse and in day-to-day interactions between groups, which defines the superior or inferior status of a group. Collaborative relations of power, on the other hand, function under the understanding that power originates in interpersonal and intergroup relations. Power is created together with others rather than imposed. Thus, Cummins' framework suggests that the micro-interactions between educators, students, and their communities are never impartial. They either reinforce coercive relations of power and disempower individuals or foster mutual relations of power. Parallel to power relations, Cummins made reference to the influence of identity on schooling. He contended that the long-term depreciation of minority students' cultural identities has strongly contributed to the students' sense of ambivalence that they feel about their identity. This insecurity leads to conflicts with teachers and resistance to academic engagement. This is especially noticeable among the Latino students in this book who are forced to struggle and choose between two worlds.

Anthropological Explanations for Differential Achievement Among Nonmainstream Groups

The field of anthropology has been concerned with examining the role of culture in education and with the manner in which social institutions affect the transmission of knowledge. In the past, cultural arguments viewed academic underachievement of nonmainstream students as being a direct result of self-perpetuating "cultures of poverty and/or cultural deprivation" (Deutsch, Bloom, Brown, Deutsch, Goldstein, John, Katz, Levinson, Peisach, & Whiteman, 1967). Understanding and discussing the phenomena of culture conflict are greatly needed when dealing with the education of ethnically diverse groups. Culture conflict, by definition, refers to interactions between members of two or more cultures; consequently, the questions of attitudes toward one's own culture or other cultures and the question of the comparative value of various cultures are involved when culture conflict is discussed.

In this book, an understanding of the concept of cultural relativism is useful in that it facilitates our interpretation of the attitudes some educators bring to the classroom regarding their own culture and the culture of the children they teach. Such attitudes sometimes lead educators to place a lower hierarchical value on the worldviews of bicultural students, their knowledge, and their interpretation of educational success. Some educators interviewed for this study entered urban classrooms with strong subtractive beliefs of the knowledge and values that minority communities and their environments exert on bicultural students.

The application of this understanding to the contemporary educational scenario provides an interesting comparison between mainstream educators and ethnic minority students. The data in this study attest that mainstream educators and school administrators of European origin are overwhelmingly well represented in urban high school classrooms in the southwestern area of the United States. The majority of these mainstream educators completed most of their education within an ethnically homogeneous setting. Their expectations for students' behaviors are therefore likely to be drawn from a limited and homogenous repertoire of behaviors. By the same token, not only their interpretations of academic success but also the ways to achieve academic success were passed onto them by monocultural frames of reference. In contrast, Latino bicultural students attending an urban public school have been exposed to a varied repertoire of behaviors and responses. These two distinctive background experiences, when in contact, can create conflict and misunderstandings between educators and students.

Social Reproduction Theories

Proponents of social reproduction theories contend that some children perform poorly in school because schools function as a "sorting mechanism," a mechanism that serves to maintain the status quo of a nonmainstream group. This argument diverts causation of educational failure from nonmainstream groups to the interaction between society and schools.

Generally, advocates of these models claim that some students are sorted toward the "right" streams or tracks (Oakes, 1985) and are given access to special kinds of knowledge (technology) whereas nonmainstream students are sorted toward less academic (vocational) programs. Once sorted and tracked, students receive very different treatment and types of instruction. Vocationally tracked students are asked to memorize and recite rote and static information whereas academically tracked students are encouraged to develop comprehension and critical thinking skills.

The insights I gained from the class analysis explanation helped explain the gap I observed among the Latino and mainstream students in Arizona schools. Carla and Manny, the two students and main actors in this book, were placed in lower track, nonintellectually stimulating classes. The educators in these classes were more concerned with addressing the affective needs of these students (through a linguistically less challenging curriculum and an obsessive emphasis on classroom management and discipline) to the exclusion of Carla's and Manny's cognitive needs. Providing a comfortable environment, or what Sharkey and Layzer (2000) called "benevolent conspiracy," was a priority for these educators over academics.

Pathologizing Student Failure: Critical Pedagogy and the Education of Latinos

The research outlined so far provides an explanatory framework for understanding bicultural students' academic underachievement. However, researchers must also contemplate ways to modify undemocratic classrooms, school organization, and institutions and policies that restrict the possibilities of success for subordinated students. Moreover, it is important to find ways to reduce the incipient solidarity and decreasing humanism in existence in some urban schools today, manifested in the "politics of success" that influence the ideology of mainstream educators interacting with other people's children (Delpit, 1995). Many educators of bicultural children define and enforce their own interpretations of educational success and negate those of bicultural students and their communities. Perspectives from critical theory address these issues and can help educators understand the contemporary political, social, and economic causes for unequal classroom outcomes.

If we understand that the persistent rejection of Latinos and other ethnic groups to adopt the cultural forms of the dominant culture (expressed and demanded by school principals and teachers to speak only English in school, be punctual, work independently, dress in generic ways, etc.) is, in fact, a form of resistance, then we can understand that school failure is more than just student deficiencies. The most prevailing and ordinary interpretation of school failure among school educators is the "deficit" model, particularly concerning issues of Latino education. Pathologizing Latino student failure places the liability on a set of traits (e.g., lack of English skills, poor value system, low self-concept, lack of role models, etc.). This attitude is alarming because school administrators, teachers, counselors, and personnel in contact with nonmainstream students are unaware of their complicity and the deep detrimental effect of their interactions.

Pathologizing school failure is part of the hidden curriculum that according to McLaren (1995) excuses teachers from their need to engage in pedagogical self-scrutiny or a critique of their individual roles within the school and the school's function within the wider society that contributes to school failure. When we pathologize school failure, we simultaneously protect the school and the society's ideology from criticism.

As I accepted a new college faculty position and moved from Arizona to Texas, I began to explore school options for my 12-year-old daughter. The public middle school in my new neighborhood, the one that my bilingual daughter would attend, was perceived by the community as an excellent school because of its high student standardized test scores. The school has a large 1,500 middle-class student body in which 56% of the students are of Latino origin. I met with the middle-aged Latina principal and inquired about the reason behind the school's success. She quickly responded that the academic success of her school was due to the absence of a bilingual program. She added that most of her students spoke English and that those who did not were quickly given accelerated private English language courses paid by the parents. For this neoconservative school administrator, the inability to speak proficient English was equivalent to school failure. Teenagers who entered her middle school without English proficiency appeared in her eyes as intellectually inferior and doomed to failure. For this school administrator, bilingual programs were considered lower standard programs to accommodate "inferior" races.

The myth of the inferiority of nonmainstream students' culture and language becomes part of a racist social perspective that is unfortunately very prevalent in schools serving bicultural students. Denying a bicultural student the right to express freely the adherence to his or her heritage language as an expression of identity is defining school success solely through a dominant ideological correctness. This is the myth of the cultural deprivation argument that according to McLaren (1995) explains educational problems in terms of students' failure to "fit" into the dominant mainstream world. As a result, economically disadvantaged and linguistically diverse students are labeled *at risk, deviant,* or *dropouts* when they do not behave in the way expected by their school teachers. The cultural deficit explanations of school failure, however, cannot justify why these deficiencies are consistently grouped along color and class lines.

It is of key importance for teachers to understand that school failure (and school success) is culturally mediated so they can act inside their classrooms and outside their schools in support of social, economic, and educational justice. In order to act while linking critical theory to practice, it is first necessary to revisit and redefine the meaning of pedagogy. As Giroux (1992) stated, "Pedagogy is less about providing a universalized set of prescriptions than it is about rewriting the relationship between theory and practice as a form of cultural politics" (p. 3). Cultural politics, he explained, is understood as the mechanisms that schools utilize to inculcate a meritocratic and individualistic system that perpetuates inequality, racism, and competitiveness as well as cultural ethnocentrism. In this view, schooling is analyzed as an historical process that recreates relations of power and privileged knowledge. Giroux (1992) suggested that cultural politics simultaneously maintained the status quo and supported the transmission of the "culture of silence."

For Freire (1970), the culture of silence constitutes the state of apathy and ignorance of oppressed groups which, he says, is a direct result of their condition of economic, social, and political domination.

> The oppressed suffer from a duality which has established itself in their innermost being. They discover that without freedom they cannot exist authentically, but they fear it. They are at one and the same time themselves and the oppressor whose consciousness they have internalized. (p. 33)

As oppressed and colonized groups, Latino populations form part of the "culture of silence." The duality of thought and action of the oppressed to which Freire referred is true for some Latino students. Latinos and other subordinate groups have internalized and have accepted as valid the negative opinions that mainstream groups hold about their culture and language. This encourages the self-depreciation that contributes to their withdrawal and educational failure. On the other hand, as they are forced to adopt a new identity, they learn to admire a new way of life. This results in alienation from their cultural roots and language and the formation of a confused identity.

A fundamental dimension of Freire's (1970) theory of oppressive action underscores how alienated people are easier to keep divided and controlled. For instance, Latinos' limited knowledge about the importance of bilingual education works in the interest of dominant groups. Economically dominant groups have found a way to preserve the status quo in the Latino community by keeping it divided and controlled. Freire's theories help us understand the historical hegemonic practices of "divide and rule." They also help us to understand how each individual also has the ability to "read" his or her world in a critical way (Freire & Macedo, 1987). By understanding this social construction through "reading the world," Latino students in this study may be able to understand the constraints that limit their self-affirmation. Through affirming their histories and critically examining the constraints placed upon them, these students can realize the possibilities for self-empowerment and social change.

Central to the development of a critical pedagogy is the necessity to examine how pedagogy functions as a cultural practice to generate rather than merely transmit knowledge within uneven relations of power that make up teacher–student interactions (Giroux, 1992). The students' narratives in this study corroborate that how and what we teach is intimately connected not only to the various forms of social domination but also to patterns of resistance, conflict, and eventually school alienation. Furthermore, theorists from this tradition argue that what happens in the classrooms shares a direct relationship with the formation of identities and knowledge.

Giroux's (1992) words are especially valid for the Latino students in this study. As they reflected on their experiences in school, they recalled how selective forms of knowledge imparted in their classrooms attempted to shape their identities toward a uniform standard related to the mainstream social structure. What the students in this study and Giroux affirm is that education is and will be a form of political action.

Critical frameworks do not allow for neutrality in definitions and explanations of schooling. Pedagogy is not a neutral process; therefore, *democracy, equal opportunity,* and *educational success* are terms conceptualized differently and in accordance with personal and political orientations. Educators and researchers from the critical pedagogy tradition challenge contemporary beliefs that schools function to develop an egalitarian and democratic social order. Moreover, they also question the assumptions that these institutions promote educational success for all, and as a result, social and economic mobility. Rather, they contend that schools not only do not provide opportunities for self-empowerment for subordinate groups but, rather, act to facilitate educational success as well as positive economic and social returns from schooling only for privileged groups.

This was found to be especially true for the Latino students in this study. As members of a subordinate and assimilated group, Latino students are excluded and maintained in marginalized positions in democracy. As the right to affirm their identity through their language and culture is denied, their "mass exodus" (Fine, 1991) continues.

Enacting critical pedagogy is developing voice and social empowerment reciprocally. In this context, the Latino students who are the focus of this study discovered the possibility of voicing their specific encounters, struggles, and engagements that transformed and shaped their worlds. They found an access to a forum whereupon they exposed their personal interpretation of educational success and equal opportunity as well as revealed the policies and practices that shaped their realities.

The issue of voice is a concept vital to self-empowerment and emancipation. Having voice is an expression of an impetus for healthy identity and an expression of strong culture. As they struggled with the system and engaged in dialogue with school authorities, they demonstrated that they could transform their lives and reverse their patterns of failure.

The constraints and factors contributing to the continuing underachievement of Latinos must be examined not on the basis of individual or cultural deficiencies but on the socio-cultural institutions and policies that influence individual and collective action as well as the cultural incongruities between educators and students and their respective interpretations of educational success.

The theoretical frameworks in this chapter strongly indicate that academic success transcends intragroup distinctions and fixed typologies, but they also have more to do with the negotiation of students' identities in institutional settings. They are more closely related to teacher and student ideologies and with allowing individuals to define success in their own terms. The latter forces seem to have a more pragmatic value, as they offer possibilities of reversal in the pattern of failure.

CHAPTER

2 ¿Que Pasa? Latinos: From the Most Numerous to the Most Neglected

The National Reality

We all know that the United States is undergoing a vast demographic transformation. According to the 2000 national census, the number of Hispanics in the United States increased in significant numbers. According to the census office, the proportion of the United States' population that is Hispanic is officially almost equal to the proportion that is African American. In addition to the fact that two states already have ethnic minorities as majority populations, experts predict that by 2050 one of every two Americans will be non-White. Hodgkinson (1999) also reported that 90% of all Hispanics are concentrated in 10 states and that by the year 2025 California alone will add 12 million more Hispanics. Texas and Florida will add another 8 million Latinos to the national population.

This revealing data, indicating the potential for Latinos to become even more numerous in the next few years, has caused great paranoia among politicians, policy makers, business owners, school administrators, and government officials alike. But the growing numbers of Latinos in the United States have not inspired our national or local governments to implement substantial appropriate changes responsive to the substandard living conditions of thousands of Latinos who have no health insurance, are segregated in poverty stricken barrios, and attend underfunded, crowded schools. On the contrary, the federal government's response has consisted primarily in the hiring of hundreds of new border patrol agents and in making the United States–Mexico border a "war zone." The message that is sent to Latino communities, through the border paranoia and the proliferation of "English only" laws, is a clear message of rejection of their language, culture, and values, manifested in the obsessive fear of losing a national identity and political power.

In the midst of this hostile environment and political fear lies the future of thousands of American-Mexican youth who are authentic miracles in progress. The Annie E. Casey Foundation (Chase, 2000) has reported that

23

ethnically diverse populations suffer numerous *at-risk* factors. According to the study, most children have only one parent in the home, the head of household is not a high school graduate, the family income is below the poverty line, parents do not hold a full-time, year-round job, and families chronically depend on public assistance. Most educators in the United States are well aware that these factors apply to all minorities in the United States but especially to growing numbers of Latino families.

On the academic front, Latinos today are not doing any better than they did a decade ago. Their academic achievement has remained static and very little progress is shown in high school completion rates across the country. The National Center for Educational Statistics (NCES, 2001) states that high school completion rates have steadily increased for Whites and Black young adults from 1972 through 2000, but high school completion for Latinos has not shown much improvement (see Figure 2.1).

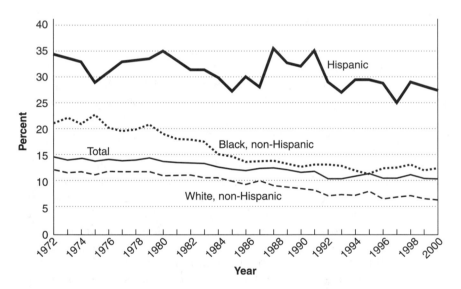

FIGURE 2.1   Status Dropout Rates of 16- Through 24-Year-Olds, by Race/Ethnicity: October 1972 through October 2000

Note. Due to small sample sizes, American Indians/Alaska Natives and Asians/Pacific Islanders are included in the total but are not shown separately. In addition, the erratic nature of the Hispanic status rates reflects, in part, the small sample size of Hispanics in the CPS. Numbers for years 1987 through 2000 reflect new editing procedures instituted by the U.S. Census Bureau for cases with missing data on school enrollment items. Numbers for years 1992 through 2000 reflect new wording of the educational attainment item in the CPS beginning in 1992. Numbers for years 1994 through 2000 reflect changes in the CPS due to newly instituted computer-assisted interviewing and the change in population controls used in the 1990 Census-based estimates, with adjustment for undercounting in the 1990 Census. See appendix D for a fuller description of the impact of these changes on reported rates.

Source: U.S. Department of Commerce, U.S. Census Bureau, Current Population Survey, October (1972–2000).

High school completion rates represent the proportion of 18- through 24-year-olds, who have completed a high school diploma or the General Development (GED) credential. Figure 2.1 shows that trends for each ethnic group have remained fairly similar over the last 29 years. While White and African-American youngsters exhibit a positive trend (and the gap between these two groups appears to have narrowed), Hispanics have not shown much progress. While completion rates rose slightly from the early 1970s to the late 1980s, they remained fairly constant during the 1990s and beyond, particularly for Latino populations. The NCES (2001) also provides us with a look at each ethnic group's educational progress for the year 2000. For example, in 2000, 64.1% of all Hispanics completed secondary schooling. This compares to 91.8% of White, 83.7% of Black, and 94.6% of Asian/Pacific Islander youngsters (see Table 2.1).

TABLE 2.1   High School Completion Rates and Number and Distribution of Completers Ages 18–24 Not Currently Enrolled in High School or Below, by Background Characteristics: October 2000

Characteristic	Completion Rate	Population (thousands)	Number of Completers (thousands)	Percent of All Completers
Total	86.5	25,138	21,743	100.0
Sex				
Male	84.9	12,460	10,580	48.7
Female	88.1	12,678	11,164	51.3
Race/Ethnicity[a]				
White, non-Hispanic	91.8	16,502	15,145	69.7
Black, non-Hispanic	83.7	3,582	2,999	13.8
Hispanic	64.1	3,797	2,433	11.2
Asian/Pacific Islander	94.6	1,074	1,016	4.7
Age				
18–19	84.0	6,718	5,645	26.0
20–21	86.4	7,363	6,359	29.2
22–24	88.1	11,057	9,739	44.8
Region				
Northeast	89.1	4,265	3,799	17.5
Midwest	88.9	5,861	5,209	24.0
South	84.4	8,895	7,506	34.5
West	85.5	6,117	5,230	24.1

Note. Because of rounding, detail may not add to total.

[a]Due to small sample sizes, American Indians/Alaska Natives are included in the total but are not shown separately.

Source: U.S. Department of Commerce, U.S. Census Bureau, Current Population Survey, October 2000.

It is important to highlight the steady improvement of African-American youth at the national level. The data show that African-American youth are reducing the gap with Whites in educational attainment marks, particularly during the 1990s. Table 2.1 also provides statistical information on high school completion by region. The southern and western regions, which normally have the highest numbers of ethnically diverse school-age population, continue to be last in high school completion rates. The report concludes that a net increase of about 3 percentage points (across groups) over 29 years represents slow progress toward improving the national high school completion rate.

Current National Dropout Figures

It is a well supported concern that far too many students drop out of high school (Finn, 1987; Kominsky, 1990). Some studies report that high school dropouts cost the United States taxpayers over $75 billion dollars each year in welfare benefits and tax revenues (Kunisawa, 1988). The losses are not only monetary. Dropping out of school may also mean higher mortality rates and more admissions to health centers, hospitals, and prisons. A highly industrialized nation such as the United States that aspires to lead the global economy into the twenty-first century and to make significant advances in technology and science cannot afford to maintain an unskilled and uneducated labor force. The National Center for Education Statistics (2001) found that dropouts usually come from low-income, single-parent families that are likely to be members of a minority group. The report indicates that over the last decade between 347,000 and 544,000 tenth- through twelfth-grade students have left school each year without completing high school. In October 2000 alone, approximately 3.8 million young adults did not complete high school. These adolescents accounted for 10.9% of the 34.6 million 16- through 24-year-olds in the United States in 2000. There has been no improvement in the dropout rates since the decline from the early 1970s into the late 1980s.

As we see in Table 2.2, the difference between the rates for Whites and African Americans has narrowed. However, most gains for African Americans occurred during the 1970s and 1980s with the gap remaining constant in the 1990s. As to the Latinos in the United States, the figures show no significant progress. Latinos continue to have a high status dropout rate when compared to that of Asians, Whites, or Blacks. In 2000, the status dropout rate for Hispanics was 27.8% compared to 3.8% for Asian/Pacific Islanders, 6.9% for Whites, and 13.1% for African Americans (NCES, 2001).

Thus, Latinos as a group are more likely to be high school dropouts than any other ethnic group. As this report indicates, during this 29-year period, 3 out of every 10 Hispanic students were reported to be out of school and lacking a high school credential. Even when the proportion of Hispanic students was very similar to that of Blacks (15.1% and 14.6%, respectively), Hispanics

TABLE 2.2 Status Dropout Rates and Number and Distribution of Dropouts of 16- Through 24-Year-Olds, by Background Characteristics: October 2000

Characteristic	Status Dropout Rate (percent)	Number of Status Dropouts (thousands)	Population (thousands)	Percent of All Dropouts	Percent of Population
Total	10.9	3,776	34,568	100.0	100.0
Sex					
Male	12.0	2,082	17,402	55.1	50.3
Female	9.9	1,694	17,166	44.9	49.7
Race/ethnicity[a]					
White, non-Hispanic	6.9	1,564	22,574	41.4	65.3
Black, non-Hispanic	13.1	663	5,058	17.6	14.6
Hispanic	27.8	1,456	5,237	38.6	15.1
Asian/Pacific Islander	3.8	54	1,417	1.4	4.1
Age					
16	3.9	153	3,887	4.1	11.2
17	7.6	307	4,023	8.1	11.6
18	11.6	468	4,019	12.4	11.6
19	13.5	544	4,026	14.4	11.6
20–24	12.4	2,304	18,613	61.0	53.8
Recency of immigration					
Born outside the 50 states and the District of Columbia					
Hispanic	44.2	1,007	2,282	26.7	6.6
Non-Hispanic	7.4	140	1,907	3.7	5.5
First generation[b]					
Hispanic	14.6	244	1,669	6.5	4.8
Non-Hispanic	4.6	84	1,837	2.2	5.3
Second generation or more[c]					
Hispanic	15.9	205	1,286	5.4	3.7
Non-Hispanic	8.2	2,096	25,586	55.5	74.0
Region					
Northeast	8.5	504	5,945	13.3	17.2
Midwest	9.2	741	8,058	19.6	23.3
South	12.9	1,597	12,337	42.3	35.7
West	11.3	933	8,228	24.7	23.8

Note. Because of rounding, detail may not add to total.

[a]Due to small sample sizes, American Indians/Alaska Natives are included in the total but are not shown separately.

[b]Individuals defined as "first generation" were born in the 50 states or the District of Columbia, and one or both of their parents were born outside the 50 states or the District of Columbia.

[c]Individuals defined as "second generation or more" were born in the 50 states or the District of Columbia, as were both of their parents.

Source: U.S. Department of Commerce, U.S. Census Bureau, Current Population Survey, October 2000.

were over-represented among status dropouts in 2000. A total of 1.5 million Hispanics were dropouts in 2000, representing 27.8% of all Hispanic young adults (NCES, 2001).

In addition, the NCES report also reveals significant distinctions that exist among the various groups that make up the Latino population. The data are analyzed within three groups of Latino populations: foreign-born Latinos, first-generation Hispanics, and second-generation Hispanics. The report reveals that foreign-born Latinos are more likely to be dropouts: 44.2% of Hispanic young adolescents born outside the United States were high school dropouts. Hispanics born in the United States were less likely to be dropouts.

This data set seems to contradict earlier influential theories of minority students' academic engagement (Ogbu, 1978, 1983, 1985). The report indicates that the foreign-born (voluntary) Latinos drop out and become academically disengaged in much higher numbers than do domestic (involuntary) Latinos born in the United States. However, both groups represent the most at-risk population in the United States public education system today.

As we know, the twenty-first century has faced us with new realities of previously unknown challenges. We have entered a period marked by dynamic processes of globalization, high mobility of material and human resources, and a massive influx of modern technologies in all spheres of life. Today, a high school diploma constitutes a minimal requirement for admittance into the labor market. As the NCES report suggests, Latino students are more likely than any other ethnic group to be unemployed, receive public assistance, and populate the nation's prisons.

In the Introduction to this book, I mentioned that while teaching at a higher learning institution in the southwest United States in the mid-1980s, I was appalled by the handful of Latino students enrolled in college undergraduate and graduate programs in most fields of knowledge. I was disturbed by the sheer inequity in the low Latino student college enrollment in the southwestern United States, given that the Mexican origin population is the largest ethnic group. As I started to work in public high schools in the 1990s, I began to realize the multifaceted factors that play out in the decisions Latino students make on their schooling. As we will see later in the book, these factors are multiple and intricately complex. They range from the placement of Latino students in segregated and culturally incongruent educational programs to the inexplicable unequal ratio between Latino teachers and their students and to the emotionally damaging classroom interactions between teachers and bicultural students. There are still thousands of Mexican-American students who never graduate from either a traditional high school or alternative schools. As I observed throughout my 17 years of residence in Arizona, only a few Latino students were eligible to attend a university if they managed to graduate. In Texas where I currently reside, former governor George W. Bush implemented strict high school graduation requirements through the development of the Texas Academic Assessment Standards (TAAS), a uniform high stakes test that costs millions of dollars to implement. After several years of new standards and rigorous testing, however, the dropout figures for Mexican youth in Texas indicate that there has been no apparent improvement (Romo & Falbo, 1996). The Latino student dropout rate remains not only unacceptably high, but student performance rates are also the lowest in all measures of academic progress. Valenzuela's (1999) ethnographic study in a Houston high school found that for every 1,200 to 1,500 high school freshman enrolled, only 400 to 500 students graduate. As Valenzuela's research indicates, the Texas educational authorities seem to view a 48% school district dropout rate as normal.

The Arizona Reality

Conservative voters, supported by the political campaign financed by California millionaire Ron Unz, resulted in the passage of Proposition 203 in Arizona in an attempt to eliminate bilingual education from its schools. Arizona was split generally along racial lines, 64% mostly Anglo residents supporting the measure and 36% mostly Hispanic residents opposing it (Bodfield, 2000). Most of the politically driven advocates for the dismantling of bilingual education were residents of wealthier suburbs while the supporters of bilingualism in schools were residents of the barrios, downtown areas, Native American reservations, and vicinities located around universities. A spokesman for the organization Chicanos por la Causa claimed that the vote "smacked of racism" (Bodfield, 2000). After all, many Arizona residents were well aware that English immersion programs in the past were not the most efficient way to educate bicultural students. From 1919 to 1967 Arizona utilized the "1-C" English immersion program to educate Hispanic students not proficient in English. During that time, graduation rates for Hispanics never rose above 40% (Gonzalez & Melis, 2000).

In Arizona as a whole, only a small number of children are enrolled in bilingual programs. In the large school district where this study took place, no more than 20% of Mexican origin children received bilingual education in schools. The low number of bicultural students enrolled in transitional bilingual programs in Arizona may, in fact, explain why Latinos in the state still suffer the highest attrition. If these conditions prevail, the academic improvement of Mexican youth in Arizona will probably be a pipe dream in the years to come. Many dedicated educators know that the psychological empowerment that bilingual programs offer children often become the sole reason bicultural students persevere and stay in school (Aparicio, 2000). In spite of the numerous research studies that demonstrate the psycho-social benefits behind bilingual programs (Cummins 1989, 1996; Krashen, 1991) and as the testimonies of the students in this study will corroborate, these programs have begun a steady dismantling in Arizona's schools. In the large southern Arizona urban school district where this study took place, the dropout rate was significantly cut when comprehensive bilingual education was implemented. The dropout rate for ninth-graders went from 16% to 5% [National Clearinghouse for Bilingual Education (NCBE), 2001]. After the passing of Proposition 203, funding for these programs will be severely affected.

Some of the main reasons behind academic disengagement can be traced directly to the reduced number of Latino students in Arizona who are served with bilingual education programs, the transitional quick-exit nature of these programs, and the lack of funding for the training of existing bilingual teachers and recruitment of new ones. The Arizona Department of Education 1999–2000 Dropout Rate report (see Table 2.3) explains why Arizona's schools continue to get an "F" in educating Latino children.

In Table 2.3, the enrollment count, the dropout count, and the dropout rate are each shown by grade. For example, in the 1999–2000 academic year, 71,188 Latino high school students enrolled in Arizona's schools. Of that, 10,969 students were officially reported as dropouts by local school districts, which resulted in a 15.4% dropout rate for Hispanic high school students. This figure places Latinos again as the group with the second highest attrition rate in the state, preceded only by Native Americans, many of whom have blood and cultural ties with Latinos in Arizona.

The failure of Latinos has not improved even slightly since the release of the unabridged study on Arizona educational demographics (Hodgkinson, 1996). According to this study, Arizona ranked forty-sixth in the nation in terms of the chance that a 19-year-old Latino might one day attend college. It also acknowledged the state as having the second highest dropout rate in the nation (after Louisiana) as well as the first place nationally for both school absenteeism and teen pregnancy.

In response to these unfavorable ratings, Arizona school districts' dropout intervention programs proliferated in the 1990s. In desperate attempts to show that progress was being made, urban public schools, forsaking quality, continued to "socially promote" ill-prepared students. This was abetted by offering multiple remedial programs for the so called at-risk students. Instruction tailored for teenage mothers and adolescents on probation and even federal programs that offer economic compensation for those who graduate (measures in some countries that could be seen as extreme) were among the interventions being tried.

There are others who believe that creating new schools are better alternatives to the failing public school system. A local newspaper reported that Arizona leads the nation in classroom experiments and that alternative schools have rapidly multiplied. The article informs us that over the last two years more charter schools have been started in Arizona than in any other state in the nation. Critics claim that this is creating "an out of control alternative school system" (Tapia, 1997). It remains to be seen whether or not the rapidly growing numbers of charter schools in Arizona will outperform

TABLE 2.3   **Arizona 1999–2000 Enrollment Count, Dropout Count, and Dropout Rate by Race/Ethnicity and Grade**

Grade/Category	White	Drops	%	Hispanic	Drops	%
7	35,071	615	1.8%	22,268	930	4.2%
8	35,191	650	1.8%	20,933	979	4.7%
Total Elementary	70,262	1,265	1.8%	43,201	1,909	4.4%
9	36,468	2,336	6.4%	22,190	2,799	12.6%
10	31,414	2,369	7.5%	17,721	2,703	15.3%
11	29,549	2,477	8.4%	14,359	2,280	15.9%
12	28,303	2,346	8.3%	13,301	2,020	15.2%
Ungraded Secondary	3,769	1,003	26.6%	3,617	1,167	32.3%
Total High School	129,503	10,531	8.1%	71,188	10,969	15.4%
Total All Grades	199,765	11,796	5.9%	114,389	12,878	11.3%

Grade/Category	Native American	Drops	%	Black	Drops	%
7	4,951	303	6.1%	3,117	130	4.2%
8	4,672	335	7.2%	2,975	122	4.1%
Total Elementary	9,623	638	6.6%	6,092	252	4.1%
9	5,968	1,197	20.1%	3,292	319	9.7%
10	4,312	691	7.5%	2,577	300	11.6%
11	29,549	462	8.4%	2,299	272	11.8%
12	28,303	389	8.3%	2,200	315	14.3%
Ungraded Secondary	3,769	180	26.6%	775	240	31.0%
Total High School	129,503	2,919	16.8%	11,143	1,446	13.0%
Total All Grades	27,041	3,557	13.2%	17,235	1,698	9.0%

Grade/Category	Asian	Drops	%
7	1,220	17	1.4%
8	1,184	8	0.7%
Total Elementary	2,404	25	1.0%
9	1,328	44	3.3%
10	1,135	46	4.1%
11	1,189	55	4.6%
12	1,111	66	5.9%
Ungraded Secondary	104	21	20.2%
Total High School	4,867	232	4.8%
Total All Grades	7,271	257	3.5%

traditional schools that have more support in terms of funding and services. Nonetheless, the rapidly growing charter schools in Arizona, the crowded public schools, the long-term conservative leadership of the state, and the general public (who recently helped pass a tax increase for schools) appear to be all in agreement that something needs to be done quickly to improve the educational outcome of Arizona's children.

Latinos in Arizona

As a former school practitioner involved in the education of high school age bicultural adolescents, I observed that innovative intervention programs resulted in progress with certain nonmainstream groups in Arizona. In the last decade, there has been a romanticized but growing interest in the cultures, languages, and education of indigenous groups in Arizona. This is reflected in the growing numbers of Native American counselors hired in K–12 schools and in colleges around the state and in the number of mainstream university students majoring in Native American studies or conducting research in related fields. It is also reflected in the growing number of federal, state, and county grants awarded to higher learning institutions and in the opening of new master's and doctoral programs in Native American education in the state.

Some progress is also noticeable among African American groups, including the hiring of large numbers of African American school administrators who target with greater care and accuracy the special needs of African descent students. As indicated by the reports already presented, the academic improvement among African American students is steadily increasing and in some instances is comparable to that of mainstream students, but the condition of Latinos in the state appears to have remained stagnant.

There are, for instance, still visible statistical inequalities in the hiring of minority teachers and administrators, especially those of Latino origin. The ratio of Latino school administrators at Tangerine Unified School District (TUSD, 2000) where this study took place is unequal to the growing numbers of Latino students. For instance, out of 62,793 students enrolled in TUSD during the 2000–2001 academic year, 45.51% were Latino, 41.29% were White, 6.70% were African American, 3.98% were Native American, and 2.52% were Asian. These figures placed Latinos as the most numerous student population in the Tangerine School District. At the high school level, White students represented 48.04% of the student body, Latinos followed closely with 39.35%, African Americans 6.48%, Native Americans 3.30%, and Asian Americans 2.83%.

In the 2000 Affirmation Action Plan (TUSD, 2000), school administrators hired for that year were unequally distributed and disproportionate to the students' ethnic breakdown of the district. For instance, out of 11 high school principals, 9 were White, 1 was African American, and only 1 was Hispanic.

In the assistant principal high school category the inequality is also apparent. Out of 26 assistant principals, 17 were White, 5 were African American, and only 4 were Latinos.

In terms of the educators where this study took place, the inequality in the hiring of minority teachers was also remarkable. Out of 391 female high school teachers employed, 319 were White (44.6%) and only 49 were Hispanic (6.6%). Out of 357 male high school teachers, 298 were White (37.9%) and 38 were of Latino descent (4.8%). Given the fact that secondary Latino students in the district comprised almost 40% of the student population, the ratio of Latino educators remains at unacceptable numbers.

The ethnic inequality between Latino students and teachers in large high school institutions, as the one in this study, can only make me wonder about the educational incongruities that many culturally and linguistically diverse students experience in schools. They are being taught in a language they did not learn as children and which is foreign; they are taught values which are foreign; they are taught lifestyles which are foreign, and, in addition, they are taught by human models who are foreign (Skutnabb-Kangas, 1984).

Mexican Americans, far from being considered an indigenous group in the southwestern United States, continue to undergo persistent attacks from conservative groups throughout the country (Crawford, 1992). Instead of gaining support from mainstream educators as other minorities have, Latino students and their families continue to experience a hostile judicial and legislative climate, particularly concerning issues of immigration, linguistic rights, human rights, and affirmative action (Rodriguez, 1996). Hispanic youth are over-represented in classes below grade level; their bilingualism continues to be treated as a liability instead of a rich cultural and economic resource (Ruiz, 1988); and inadequate school funding persists among "barrio" school districts (Kozol, 1992).

In conclusion, the federal and local data presented here warn our nation of a profound educational crisis affecting all ethnically diverse students. This crisis is more dramatic and detrimental for one segment of such population: students of Latino origin. Considering current trends, millions of young Latinos will have less opportunity to participate in the "American dream." If these trends are not mitigated by creating a new vision in education, this educational neglect could eventually cause a high economic toll on our nation as a whole. It could especially affect Latino communities throughout the nation and many Mexican-descent children and adolescents.

Case Studies: The Awakening of Latino Voices

Over the years we have heard many Latino adolescents speak for educational equality and opportunity. Foley (1991) documented the "vatos" (guys) academic struggles in the southern Texan valley. We have also heard these Latino voices in the influential ethnographic study of Fine (1991) in New York, in the multicultural youth in Nieto (1992), in Romo and Falbo's (1996) study of Mexican students in Austin, and in Valenzuela (1999) in Houston.

In the new millennium, two more Arizona high school Mexican-American students tell their stories and explain their perceptions of the forces that predispose their failure in educational institutions. But, in addition, they tell us why they came back to a rather hostile educational system to graduate and succeed. At the same time, we hear the voices of their teachers who in some instances corroborate the students' views and in others contradict them.

The eloquent and candid students' testimonies in this book identify and enlighten the factors that influence the motivation, persistence, and success of nonmainstream students attending public high schools. In carrying on with this inquiry, my intent was to approach a known phenomenon from a new angle. An "emic" point of view of the participants themselves and their experiences permit a deeper understanding of the role of the school and the classroom processes in nurturing, resisting, or transforming the meanings and values students bring with them to school.

Ethnographic case studies not only involve systematic, long-term observation of phenomena, they also involve holistic, deep cultural understandings of a situation under study. As Wolcott (1975) explained, "An ethnography is a cultural description which conveys how it is to walk in someone else's shoes" (p. 113). He added that researching schools must attend to what is learned inside and outside the school and what is taught formally and learned informally. This book is nested in a documentation of relevant socio-cultural factors, including the larger Mexican-American context, the history of the neighborhood, and the attitudes of parents, educators, and school administrators toward education for Latino students.

Ethnographic research also addresses issues of culture and "how" people interpret their experiences (Hammersley & Atkinson, 1983; Merriam, 1988). In this study, educators and students define their roles and understandings of what constitutes educational success. As a high school educator, I had the opportunity to participate directly and indirectly in the lives of my students. I observed their interactions with urban institutions and recorded selected critical incidents. The "learning from people" to which Spradley (1979) referred has been at the heart of my fieldwork in my role as long-term participant and observer.

This book centers around the schooling experience of two high school adolescents of Mexican descent. Of these two participants, one might be characterized as representative of a voluntary status or recent immigrant (Ogbu, 1978) and the other can be viewed as representative of an involuntary status or Latinos born in the United States. The study sought to determine what similarities and what differences exist among Latino students according to the groups with which they identify in the context of their schooling in a dominant culture institution. Further, this inquiry was extended to 33 high school educators and administrators from diverse ethnic backgrounds through an open-ended questionnaire of 12 questions. They were asked to respond to various aspects of student engagement and success in the educational process.

In constructing a cultural analysis of the dropout phenomena and the factors that influence the persistence of nonmainstream students in schools we began to ask: What are the definitions of academic and personal success held by Latino students (immigrant and American born)? What is the interpretation of academic success held by their teachers? What are the perceptions held by students and educators of the factors that constrain or enable their success and aspirations? And in what specific ways do these factors affect their ability to negotiate the educational system and resolve problems? Understanding how culturally diverse students and their teachers view success and the requirements to be successful is essential because it exposes how we do *not* view success and reveals the guidelines we give students to succeed. In this study the educators' cultural perceptions of the meaning of success were analyzed and contrasted to the Latino students' definition of success.

Research Setting

Both high schools in which this study was conducted belong to the same school district. This district has a large nonmainstream student enrollment that is predominantly Hispanic. Both students attended these schools in a city of approximately 800,000 inhabitants in the American Southwest.

The male involuntary student attended a southside predominantly Latino neighborhood school. This high school is referred to by a pseudonym, Presidio High School (PHS). Latino lower-middle-class and poor families reside within the service area of this high school. The area where the school is located is characterized by a relatively high percentage of youth gang activity.

The school was first opened to the public in 1956. Its name was approved by the school board after taking a poll among students who attended the school in 1957. According to the 1996 school district's ethnic enrollment report, out of 2,024 students enrolled in Presidio High School in 1996, 82.81% were of Latino origin. When this research study began, a new principal of African American origin was hired. The former principal, a Mexican American, was removed from his position following a controversy that held him accountable for the school's low scores on standardized tests. As a form of introduction to my new work site, the students took a special interest in familiarizing me with the school's history. Thus, I learned that students had protested and staged a walkout when the former principal administrator (an Hispanic raised in that barrio) was removed.

The second student, a female Mexican immigrant, attended a centrally located large urban institution after transferring from a rural high school. This

A typical southwestern high school.

high school is referred to by a pseudonym, Mountain High School (MHS). Mountain High School opened its doors to the community in 1924. For many years, it was the only high school in the growing community. The history of the school has been characterized by its growth and a racial population that reflects the makeup of the city. In the early 1950s, it was one of the largest schools in the nation. Currently, it is a magnet school as part of the district's efforts to comply with a desegregation order. The school enrolls 2,351 students, numbers that administrators find constitute a great management challenge.

A 1996 district's ethnic enrollment report reveals that the number of bilingual–bicultural students continues to rise annually. Currently, the district's enrollment is 57.25% Latino, 6.30% African American, 3.70% Native American, 0.94% Asian, and 31.82% White students. Mountain High School offers a full range of day and evening courses. The evening program offers vocational community-oriented courses. The research study at both schools was conducted during the 1994–1997 academic years. During those years, the school board approved my petition to transfer from Presidio High to Mountain High School's Modern Language Department.

The Participants

Individual experiences was one criterion considered in the selection of these students. Both were labeled *at risk* for school failure. Both students repre-

An ordinary day in an urban high school.

sented a wide range of background experiences, including residence in and outside the United States, gender, social class, types of schools attended, or language and cultural retention and identification. Manny is a middle-class, third-generation Mexican-American male who is bicultural but was raised monolingually. Carla is a female working-class Mexican immigrant raised in both rural and urban settings and educated in both Mexican and American educational institutions. Both students faced a wide range of difficulties in their relationship with the educational institutions they attended. Although they were considered at risk for failure and eventually dropped out of school, they both learned to maneuver their way through the system and eventually returned and graduated. Their insights, perceptions, and stories that are illustrative of the variations that exist among people with a common cultural history, language, and heritage.

Manny was selected as a result of a spontaneous encounter outside school. As we engaged in casual conversation one day, he candidly shared with me his frustrations with the educational system, accounts of his clashes with administrators, as well as his own views about personal challenges he faced in attempting to achieve an education. I was struck by his level of maturity and awareness of the issues I was attempting to explore, and therefore I was determined that he would be an ideal candidate for my study. Carla was selected through the help of a school counselor who shared with me the challenges and difficulties the student was undergoing to complete her education. Language choice was an issue with Carla. At her request, all interviews were recorded and transcribed in Spanish, the language with which she felt most familiar and comfortable.

Teacher Survey

A survey containing 12 open-ended questions (see Chapter 5) was distributed to 31 educators and 2 administrators in the same high school the students attended. The survey was a modified version of McCarty's (1991) larger qualitative study in which 100 Navajo community members participated. In my study, the survey was randomly distributed to 33 educators from a pool of almost 250 teachers in a large urban school district. The language arts building of the school, known as "main building," was the site for survey distribution. The educators who agreed to participate were for the most part English, American history, government, and math instructors. In addition, each educator upon returning the completed questionnaires agreed to participate in follow-up interviews with me in which we reviewed and expanded on the themes to which they had responded. The pool of survey participants included 3 African Americans, 7 Latinos, and 20 Anglos. This ethnic breakdown matches the composition of the district's hired personnel.

Study Limitations

A study of a small number of selective individuals of Mexican ancestry cannot be regarded as representative of the Mexican culture as a whole. Indeed, no claim is being made for representativeness even of the subcultures (American born and immigrant) of the Mexican community to which these students belong. Every single individual, however, is influenced by the culture of his or her community and his or her nation. By the same token, a study of 33 educators and their educational philosophies cannot be regarded as representative of the views of all the teaching communities of the United States.

Issues in Latino Education is a case study of individuals and their personal experiences in two urban public high schools. It is not intended to develop unusual explanations or law-like predictions of Latinos or the Mexican-American community of the southwestern United States, although the study certainly has larger implications. The study is limited by generational distinctions, place of residence, schools attended, and cultural identification influences.

It must also be acknowledged that there is great diversity in the Latino population in the United States. Although Latinos share many cultural and social similarities regardless of their origin, they are unique to themselves and their subcultures in many respects. Thus, this study should not be generalized to all other Latinos or Mexican Americans. It should, however, be understood to be an example of the multicultural diversity represented in our contemporary educational institutions.

I have tried to use the term *Latino* or *bicultural* when possible rather than *minority, Hispanic,* or *Chicano* to identify the students and educators in this study. The term *minority* does not apply to the growing Spanish-speaking population in this country, and it seems to perpetuate a deficient view. The term *Chicano* is viewed by the majority Mexican-descent population as too aggressive. And many Mexican-American groups resent the term *Hispanic,* a term that reminds them of former colonialist Castilian days. Coincidentally, it is the term dictated by the federal government to define Spanish-speaking populations in the United States.

Finally, I believe my long-term professional contact with bicultural students and my own cultural background, rather than a limitation, represented an advantage. Conducting "authentic" research, or what Swisher (1986) called an "insider approach" greatly aided my understanding of cultural issues present during data analysis. Because of my native fluency in Spanish, data collected in the students' native language did not suffer any semantic loss and were interpreted in a genuine form. My firsthand knowledge of the community was an asset that greatly assisted in documenting and interpreting these students' experiences.

CHAPTER

3 Introducing Manny: "There's More Than Whites Out Here"

It is the end of another long day at Presidio High School. I have been looking over the name roster in my grade book trying to remember the names of the 130 new students equally distributed among my Spanish, French, and English as a Second Language (ESL) classes. I suddenly realize that the dismissal bell rang an hour ago. Feelings of guilt arise as I think about my six-year-old daughter who is probably waiting patiently for my arrival at an after-school program. Crossing the long school patio of Presidio High School toward the parking lot, located in a south-side Latino neighborhood school in southern Arizona, I realize that I had left my car keys inside the locked car. I approach the auto shop where I see a few students who are working with their teacher on a van. A student walks toward me and offers to help. While walking with his tools in hand, he starts a conversation. "Are you a new teacher here?" I nod.

He proceeds to apprise me of the school's new administration. He talks about the new school principal, an African-American female who, he relates, does not like Mexicans. His expression changes when he offers that he misses the former principal, Mr. Gatelo, a Mexican American born and raised in the neighborhood who knew all the students by their first names. I learn from Manny of the students' walkout to protest his dismissal, the low scores on standardized tests (the district's rationale for Mr. Gatelo's removal), and Manny's views on Latino students' performance on such tests.

I am also struck by Manny's description of the school's complex political issues that affect the academic engagement of 68% of the student body who are of Mexican ancestry. I am struck by his level of maturity, as well as the confrontations he experienced as a result of the school's discipline policies. These made him an ideal candidate for this study.

Manny, the only child of a third-generation Mexican-American family with roots in New Mexico, was in his junior year at Presidio High when I met him. Soon after our first meeting at the auto shop, I explained to him the nature of my research project. He agreed to be interviewed but in the privacy of

One of today's Latino students.

his home rather than at school. He had been involved in several conflicts with hall monitors and disciplinary personnel who kept him after school on suspensions. As a result of these incidents, he did not enjoy the school environment any longer.

From birth, Manny has lived in a pleasant, suburban, middle-class neighborhood a few miles away from the low-income area that surrounds his school. His neighborhood represents the ethnic diversity of his school and is an area where well established Mexican-American families have lived for two decades alongside Anglo and African American families.

During my first visit to his home, I was introduced to his parents. For the last 20 years Manny's father has been employed at a national missile firm. His mother, also of Mexican heritage, was a legal secretary for the county government. Even though both parents were fluent Spanish speakers, I noticed that English was the dominant language in the household. Manny had a partial command of Spanish, which he claimed to understand but not able to speak. Manny's father had attended and graduated from Presidio High in the early 1960s. He recalled times when he was sent home or ordered to remain inside a classroom closet for speaking Spanish at school. Such painful memories kept Manny's parents from raising him bilingually. Manny's father seemed a bit embarrassed when he confided to me on one occasion, "We did not push him to speak Spanish because we did not want Manny to go through what we went through in school." Manny joins the hundreds of Mexican-descent students where the loss of Spanish is the price to pay for social integration and academic achievement.

When the parents learned I was a teacher, they eagerly volunteered information on what they believed was not working at their son's school. On two occasions, I sat and listened to Manny's mother as she insisted I needed to hear the nightmare she had gone through with the school's bureaucratic procedures and disciplinary rules. On subsequent visits to his home, I was introduced to Manny's paternal grandmother and on a different occasion to his maternal grandmother. Manny's partial understanding of Spanish was greatly due to the contact with his extended family. The concept of unity and closeness characteristic of many Latino families was very present in Manny's home environment.

Manny owned two vehicles that he drove to school, a pager, and a cellular phone. To counter the perception of wealth by his peers, Manny followed teen fashion (t-shirts, baggy pants, baseball caps) and wore old clothes to school. He did not participate in school clubs or after-school activities. He neither showed any interest in sports nor took part in school functions. He often complained that the school administration limited the students' desires as to their projects. He related that most clubs or school events were teacher oriented rather than student initiated. His involvement with school friends was outside the school environment.

Manny is able to turn old wrecks into functional and fancy models that look as if they were out of a car magazine. Although his parents discouraged him from getting a job after school, they supported his passion for remodeling cars by purchasing him a sound system that he used to earn money as a disk-jockey on weekends. Manny became his peers' favorite disc-jockey at private parties, from which he saved sufficient money to remodel his cars.

Success: The American Dream

Success for Manny revolved around the pursuit of the American dream, which for most adolescents represents financial independence, self-reliance, and freedom of movement. Thus, his definition of success is perhaps typical of American teenagers, especially the emphasis on self-reliance:

> Success means making it in life, having a car; just the American dream, making it, paying the bills, having a house. You have to work though. There's no other way around it: making it, not having to depend on anybody but yourself, success.

The financial realities of being an adult are reflected in Manny's comments about pursuing the dream: "You have to drive a car, pay your bills, pay insurance, pay this, pay that." He viewed stereotypes about Hispanics, the

advantages that Anglos have in society, and the generation gap as all potentially working against fulfillment of his version of the American dream. Manny
stated three ways to achieve the dream: "playing the game," "drugs and
crime," and "finding a financial backing to open his own enterprise."

"Playing the game" refers to education and joining a profession. To accomplish the American dream, Manny saw as one option playing the game of
school as his parents had always counseled him. Yet, Manny made it clear that
for him school was a waste of time. To him the main failing of the school was
the absence of practical knowledge. On several occasions he shared that the
school curriculum was totally disconnected from his interests and academic
curiosities. Yet he felt a great respect for his parents' views. He put it this way:

> My parents always wanted me to graduate from school. I just do it for them. I
> just don't like school at all. I did not drop out only because I didn't want to upset
> them.

Manny referred to going to school as "playing the game": following in-
structions and finally getting a professional job as a teacher or a doctor. He explained that teachers' beliefs about being successful are centered around
entering college. Common sense for Manny also meant not dropping out of
school. The alternative to being in school was to be idle. When asked why he
did not drop out, he replied:

> I did not want to upset my mom and dad. If I could breeze my way through high
> school getting C's and D's, doing whatever had to be done to pass, it was just
> common sense. A lot of my friends dropped out—they just get caught up—par-
> tying. Some of them straighten out and have gone back to school, some of them
> just do the same thing.

Manny felt that society in the United States, and in particular the media,
promotes excessive materialism and immerses people in a race to obtain the
"American dream" ideal as quickly as possible. For some, drug dealing, the
alternative to education, becomes an option to reach the dream, especially
when other options seem closed.

> Kids get caught up because we see money on TV, we see the cars, the American
> dream, and it's like if we have to go drug dealing, do whatever we have to do to
> get those things. I think kids get caught up in the same dreams—just like you
> guys [teachers] do. I can go to work right now and go buy me a car, get some
> credit, buy me a house. We are caught in the same dreams as you do.

Manny seemed well aware that his generation confronts many challenges and material temptations. He talked about students he knew at school
who got into trouble because of the need to possess material things instantly.

He felt that television had shaped his generation and that the American dream for many students consisted of possessing a mansion, cars, and name-brand equipment. He continued:

> You see it on TV, you see the brand new Lexus, the Mercedes. You want to get that before you're old and gone. Be a 60-year-old man and driving. You want to be a 13-year-old kid driving a Lexus. TV, it's pretty bad, it has shaped our generation.

Manny rejected partying all the time, a behavior of dropouts. He appeared to be aware that he was a product of the American society that has been heavily influenced by the media. But he was skeptical that through education or "playing the game" he could actually achieve the American dream. According to Manny, the biggest problem with education, aside from the everyday difficulties in his own school, was the big risk of education not actually leading to the American dream. Clearly, Manny understood what it meant to be a responsible adult and to achieve the American dream—one has to work for it.

For Manny, education or "playing the game" involved not only too much time but also long-term risk. He wanted to have money and time to enjoy the dream to its fullest, but he viewed education as the long route to accomplishing financial stability and success. He reflected:

> Even with a high school diploma, where does it get you? Not far. I see education as a gamble, life's a gamble. You go to school for 2, 4, 10 years, get the doctorate, the whole works, and you get out of school and there's too many of those people. You've wasted thousands of dollars in school; a degree doesn't guarantee you nothing. I am not saying education is a waste of time. I am saying that there is a bunch of other options. At school, they make it look like college is the only one. You can put all your time and energy to open up your own business.

For Manny, a high school and college education did not always take you where you wanted to go. He felt that in school the college option was the only one promoted. However, for those who wanted to receive any form of practical training, the approach he experienced in school was, to him, a "waste of time":

> What I got out more of high school was like graphic arts, media arts, stuff like that which I found practical. In school you don't learn much. It is a waste of time and money. You can't replace time. Once it's gone. That's it.

When Manny was asked if he considered himself successful in the school context, he replied that students had different goals. Some just wanted to graduate, some wanted to learn something practical, and some went to school without a clear goal in mind other than just to gain friends and socialize. He felt that his aspirations and goals were not met in school; therefore, he did not consider himself successful even though he was about to graduate. He summarized: "I'd get frustrated at school sometimes when all I received was inert knowledge. I wasn't able to produce things."

Time and Money: "If You Have Money, You Can Buy Time"

As mentioned above, Manny was oriented toward a practical and fast route to achieve his ideal of the American dream. His theory of education was that it should be a preparation for "real life." In his assessment of high school, he felt it had failed him because it taught him little he did not already know or little he could use in pursuing the American dream. The concepts that dominated Manny's view of the world were money and time. In terms of money, Manny admitted that it did not buy happiness but that it did buy time. He also connected the issue of money to the world of politics and the national arena by pointing out that our society is constructed squarely upon a base of money and power.

> What money gives you is time. You can pay somebody to mow the lawn, you don't have to do it. The more money I have, the more time to enjoy it. But you have to go and get it yourself. Money makes the world go round. Politics works around money, just like the kickbacks and the bribes congressmen receive for passing legislation.

Manny explained that for him school represented "a big social hour." He cited some of the ways school wasted his time. Manny noted that high school could easily be reduced to a two-year curriculum. He criticized the numerous distractions at school, especially the superficial student council activities sponsored and approved by mainstream teachers. According to Manny, these activities promoted students' overattention to the clothing they wore to school, prom parties, picture days, sport events, and homecoming events. He believed that an efficient utilization of time at school would be to take early college classes for your major while in high school, programs he knew existed in wealthier public high schools in town. Courses that were hands-on and directly related to a future occupation, he felt, would actively engage students in school. To that effect, he says:

> There are too many distractions, proms, pictures, games, sports, homecoming. They should make school a bit speedier. Not so much bull_____. Attendance was a waste of time. Teachers spend 15 minutes of class time taking attendance.

A class only lasts 50 min. You know what would work? Right when you walk in class, you should show your Arizona I.D., swipe it, punch your matric. number instead of attendance. Much faster. We have TV's, cable in every classroom. How much harder would it be to run a telephone line and hook it up to a computer? That's all you need.

Manny suggested that a way to reduce the "waste of time" would be for high schools to establish more partnerships with colleges and universities. He was well aware that wealthier public schools in suburban areas had initiated innovative partnership programs with higher learning institutions, but southside Latino barrio schools continued operating as they did 20 years ago.

When you get into college, you pick your major. But before you have to take basic courses that lead you up to that. Why can't you start that in high school? A friend I have at CDA school is taking concurrent biology and computer courses at the university. . . . Here in the southside our schools are no different than when my father attended 25 years ago.

There were a few high school classes that Manny found valuable and not a waste of time. These included printing, media arts, and graphic arts, which helped him see tangible results for his efforts. These vocational classes were taught, for the most part, by Latino bilingual educators with whom Manny felt connected. Manny talked with enthusiasm for a long time about the vocational classes. I saw a smile when he made the following comments:

Classes that taught me something were those that allowed me to make things. I had something to show. More like the feeling of "I did it." Same thing with the stereo, car, radio, graphic arts, making diplomas. In printing class, I made a bunch of diplomas for the whole school. I didn't have to earn one. I made it. I knew what kind of work went into making a diploma. It's like, you got it, you earned it, but I had a harder time making it than you probably had earning it. Not just anybody can do it. That's what makes the world go round. Different people making different things. Where are the entrepreneurs? The self-employed? You need those people in the world too.

High School Is a Joke: "It's a Mechanical Game"

For Manny, school was a "mechanical game" in which the rules consisted of just passing the class but not learning the content. He felt that teachers were always overly concerned with giving frequent weekly grades that the principal demanded. He also felt that the low standardized test scores at Presidio High (the lowest scores among the district's 12 large high schools) were a reflection of poor teaching, an uninteresting curriculum, and the mechanization of learning:

> I don't remember a bit of what they "taught" me. Teachers didn't care if you learn as long as they had a grade on paper. Then, they cared when they couldn't justify to the principal why there were so many F's. But almost everybody gets A's and B's at school. But those placement tests; they tell you what we really know. That's why we have such low scores. We don't hardly do our homework. If we do, it is mechanically. We'd copy answers from the book. Like social studies class . . . you could bull_____ your way through homework there. You didn't need to read the chapters to answer the questions. You only needed to find the words in italic.

Manny was well aware of what was needed in order "to play the game" in the mainstream educational setting. His testimony spoke of nonstimulating classes characterized by mechanization of learning and an absence of higher-order critical thinking activities. He learned to adjust to the rules set by more powerful others, even if this meant accepting situations he found disturbing. This included getting along with teachers who played favorites:

> I learned how to play the game. I just started talking to teachers, being friendly with teachers. I would often notice how they favored athletes. I'd just do my work, I knew I couldn't change things. When I started getting A's at the end of my senior year, and I didn't belong to any football team, the teachers were like "Manny is getting A's." I hate to say it, but you can just bull_____ your way through high school. It was easy. It was just a big joke.

The Big School Problem: "This Is the Twenty-First Century; There's More Than Whites Out Here"

Some of the problems Manny found with school involved its disconnection from the reality of the community and the students' experiences. He emphasized that this disconnection was a major reason behind students' lack of interest in school. School, he believed, was separated from the reality of what and how kids like to learn, including their language choice. According to him, the students' own discourse and language were not validated in school. In one of our interviews he shared that he was asked to rewrite a class project using "academic" language, not street language. The topic that Manny selected dealt with students' views on racism in schools. His elaborate book, which was neatly typed, edited, bound by himself at the print shop, and well researched, received a "D" as a final grade. Since his research topic was on students' views about racism, he included authentic testimonies and students' everyday language. The teacher felt that the paper was not entirely written in standard English and this was his main argument in justifying giving Manny a low grade. Manny was disappointed, and he felt that the teacher did not agree with his views on the subject. Issues of racism and discrimination in school were not openly discussed in this class and were considered tabu, according to Manny. He shared with me other situations in which his efforts to engage academically were not acknowledged:

> On another occasion a paper that I presented and researched at school had to do with hand guns. I made a little video to go with it and visited the library several times but the teacher put restrictions on the way I could present the paper to the class: "You can't cuss, you can't use your normal language." For us, that is normal talk. It comes out naturally. I don't mean slip out the way we talk on the streets, everybody cussing, and when it slips out at school—BUM! You get detention. It is no-cussing explicit things. It is the generation gap with the teachers.

Manny's words here made me reflect on Anzaldua's (1999) analysis on Chicano border tongues. According to this feminist Chicana author, people who live in a country in which Spanish is not the official language and who cannot identify with standard English need a language they can connect to their identity, a language in which they can "communicate the realities and values true to themselves—a language with terms that are neither Spanish nor English but both" (p. 77).

Many Mexican Americans in schools feel the need to identify themselves as distinct individuals through their own linguistic forms. They need to use a language close to their heart and to their identity, a language that is not understood and often denied in dominant mainstream institutions. Corson (1999) argued that the impact of stereotypes can greatly affect a teacher's judgment of the student's academic potential. Language is usually the first indicator teachers use to judge such potential. Attitudes toward nonstandard speech influence teachers' expectations and have little to do with students' intellectual capabilities.

Manny perceived the school as embodying irrelevant content, wasted time, as well as a disconnection between teaching his values and those taught there. Manny elaborated:

> I always found that those few teachers that make learning fun, related learning with to real life stuff, not just textbook stuff 'cause those are words in a book not real life. . . . We are growing up in different times. Most of our generation are dying, killed by drugs, gangs, teen pregnancy. Teachers have lived longer lives, but we're growing up in totally different surroundings. Teachers don't know the reality that surrounds the school, the neighborhood. I keep telling myself, "You will only have to be with them for four years not the rest of your life." You have to just tell yourself: "These people are full of s_____; they don't know what I've been through."

Manny's words clearly reveal his frustration when he did not find the school curricula in tune with the reality of the students and their communities. Manny proceeded to tell me his experience in science classes. He felt that "school kills your natural curiosity" by restricting knowledge to a prescribed book. The mechanical, rote learning approach paralyzed the students' ability to think critically and explore new options. He added:

> In school, science is like "look this is how it is in the book." It don't matter what you think. It's written and proven. If it's written and proven, why am I sitting in this class? There's no room to think. They kill your natural curiosity. In chemistry, maybe we add a bit more baking soda or ammonia just to see what happens. Forget the formula. We want to see new things, create our own even if we make mistakes in the process. Why is it that everything has to be so controlled by the books?

His assessment of the school curriculum led him to reflect on his experience in history and American government classes in which he found that "history was only presented from the White man's perspective." With these words Manny expressed the factors that contributed to students' opposition and academic disengagement. Manny's voice here is a powerful indicator that when students of color do not see themselves represented in the curriculum, or when the representation is selective, a painful feeling of cultural isolation develops. A strong message is sent, a message that not only portrays a racial hierarchy among races but also fosters a sense that "school is meaningless." Manny's words seem to imply that by ignoring the historical contributions of diverse communities to the making of the nation, schools contributed to the gradual academic disengagement of minority students. Manny said:

> History was a big waste of time for me. Mr. O'Rourke was the teacher of that class. We had to take history one whole year. There was a couple of little Hispanic things in the book, a couple of Indian things treated very superficially and we spent not more than a few minutes on them. Most of the time, it was more like: "The Indians slaughtered this person and that one," and I'd go "What?" "This is bull_____." From then on, I didn't pay attention. I didn't care for the class. I knew already what the teacher was going to say. All we talked about was the White man's struggle and the White men did this, and the White men did that. It's like you know what? It's the twenty-first century; there's a lot more than Whites out here.

When I asked Manny why he did not challenge the content of the curriculum, he replied that he had tried it once and got into trouble. He preferred to pretend he was enjoying the class. His words are a reflection of the cultural isolation and powerlessness bicultural students encounter in high school. He related:

I thought I was already in enough trouble. I'd better sit and pretend I am enjoying this, or do something else. Inside of me I'd go, "Why do I want to learn about the White people? That's not where I came from."

During his junior year, Manny received disciplinary referrals from his science teacher, an older man who soon retired. The referrals were due to Manny's "excessive talking" in class. As he confided, "There were too many interesting people in that class, and the lectures were boring." Manny described his teacher as "a nice old man, I got a good grade in his class though." He was ordered to attend the after-school detention program. Manny did not enjoy remaining at school one minute past the dismissal bell. Therefore, after ignoring after-school detention twice, he received 21 days of in-school suspension. During that same year, he also got involved in two other incidents with substitute teachers that resulted in additional suspensions. According to Manny, one of the substitute teachers not only attempted to twist his arm but also pushed him. In 13 years of schooling, Manny was suspended for a total of approximately three-quarters of a year. In one of our interviews he revealed that his grades were far better during in-house suspensions than when he was in regular school: He said:

> If I could have school my way, I'd do what I did when I was on in-school suspension. I'd do what I have to do, my assignments, my work, cut out all the bull_____ classes. That's how I learned most of my school stuff, by myself. Writing and reading, doing math. You don't really need a teacher. In-school suspension, I got better grades than in the classroom.

In his view, Manny is different from the students who dropped out because of disciplinary actions:

> I'd rather hand in my work. Besides, I don't have to put up with no people [other students] yelling, cussing, people that don't want to learn, just all the bull_____. I'd just give my work and that's it; that's the difference between me and the people who drop out.

The statements above clearly indicate Manny's dissatisfaction with the public school system. His classes were filled with students with multiple emotional and social distractions and disturbances that eventually stamped out the students' desire to learn. Manny preferred to work independently rather than be subjected to such a classroom environment.

Identity: "I Don't Fit in Here, and I Don't Fit in There"

Identity was a dominant theme across most of the conversations in our interviews. Manny spoke often of his struggle and confusion to define himself. In his initial self-reflections, Manny revealed the typical confusion of Chicano and Mexican American ethnicity. By the end of our interview on the topic, however, his statements manifested his allegiance to his Mexican ancestry. My first question on the topic puzzled him:

> Who am I? I don't know—that's kind of a hard question to answer. Who am I? I'm a person, a name, a social security, just like everybody else. I don't know how to explain it. I'm a Mexican. I'm a Mexican American. I don't fit in over here and I don't fit over there.

I asked him to elaborate on his statement "I don't fit in over here and I don't fit over there." He explained:

> Well, sometimes I think Mexican kids don't like me. At school, some of them do, you know. Sometimes it is hard getting along. I think it is just communication, language problems. But I'm Mexican, I can speak some Spanish, I can talk to those people. I've never gotten in a fight with them. I know Mexican girls, I have friends.

I asked him to tell me about here.

> Here, it's just like, you're Mexican. They treat you the same way as the other Mexicans over there. It's like you want to tell them, "Hey, you know I was born here!" But it's just who I am. I don't know, I can't explain it. But that's a different question. You are asking me who am I? I am a Mexican American, I am smart. I consider myself smart not dumb. I don't know physically. I am a bit short. That's about it. I've never thought about it.

I sensed the tension in his voice when he started to talk about the very personal issue of his confusing sense of ethnicity. Manny's ambivalent feelings about his identity seem to be common to many Latinos in the United States. Stavans (1995) called it the *bifocal identity*, an accepted ambiguous process of self-discovery embraced by most Latinos living in a world of cultural contradictions and negative messages society in the United States sends. Nevertheless, Manny adhered to his Mexican ancestry. He did not hide it or deny it. Instead, he challenged the views of society and clearly identified himself with more recent immigrants. His words do not reflect Ogbu's (1978) distinction between domestic caste-like and immigrant minorities:

> They look at me as if I were from the other side. No, I mean, I don't really care what people think. But it's just the way people see you. They make you feel you don't belong. You know what I mean? Where you came from? Mexico. It's from Mexico. I know I came from there somewhere along the line but after so many generations. I came from the same place that the people are coming right now. It's just that my family came before. I belong here, I know I do, but I just can't

explain the way people think. When they stare at you or say, "Look at that wet-back!" or "Look at that Mexican!" It hurts, but I really don't care.

Manny did demonstrate a strong sense of caring. While he talked, he let his anger out and vented the sense of embarrassment, shame, and confusion he was made to feel about his heritage by the dominant society. To be told that you come from "the other side" is synonymous with being told you come from an inferior place. That is the message Manny said he has always received. Manny's bicultural identity cannot be easily categorized. He did not reject or try to hide the Latino aspects of his heritage nor did he spend much time in school with Anglo friends. Most of the friends he socialized with were also Mexican Americans. Rebelling against dominant society messages of inferiority, Manny refused to hide his ethnic heritage. Even though he could not claim a direct allegiance to one single ethnic group, Manny clearly rejected racist views:

> At school, it was weird. I told you before I really didn't want to be there. Like, Ken is a friend of mine, he is African American, and his father is friends with Ms. Robertson [referring to the African American principal whom Manny perceived as racist]. When she saw us together once, she called him and said, "Does your father know who are you hanging around with?" and she went on, this and that. What if I was Black? Would that change anything? I think it was because I was Mexican why she said that.

In spite of his attempts to defend his identity, Manny was convinced that his ethnicity in this society is a liability. That was the message he received from school authorities and society in general. He felt he was not alone, and he expressed similarities he perceived with other minorities. I asked him what he felt were the differences between him and an African American or an Anglo person. He answered:

> Between me and an African American person? There are no differences except the skin. We probably think about the same. Between me and an Anglo? That's where it gets a little different. To me being White, it just gives you more chances. White people are not stereotyped right away as I am. They look at a Mexican and they think "drug dealer," "gang member."

At the same time, Manny was well aware of social and class distinctions:

> But I know some White people where I live. We know each other for a long time. We grew up together in the same neighborhood and they think the same as me. You, anybody from the other side of town though, the rich part, same age and everything, and they see things a lot different.

His personal philosophy in relation to ethnic equality is clearly reflected in this statement:

This society is trying to say that everyone is treated equal. But when you really think about it—the Constitution wasn't written for you and me. It was meant for rich, White, Anglo land-owner people.

Identity is the crux of Manny's criticism of his high school experience. He recalled that the only validation of his Latino identity was when he enrolled in a Southwestern literature class that allowed him to learn about his Mexican background. As he said, it was "the only class I loved in school." Other definite identification and allegiance with his ethnicity were evident when he talked about this class and his teacher, Mr. Galvan, a Latino role model who knew how to present Manny's culture in a positive way. Manny's voice turned lively and enthusiastic:

> Mr. Galvan, that teacher was the greatest teacher. I love this teacher and I will never forget him. He taught us about Mexicans, where we came from, stuff that was important to us, our history. I mean, I don't care where some White people came from. Who would care less? They don't do nothing for me. I want to know what my people went through. That was the one and only class I really loved. I took it one time and that was the only time I could take it. He talked about the old city and the barrios. It was a fun class. That's the class I liked.

Manny then told me about the school principal's removing this class from the curriculum and assigning Mr. Galvan to a new project with the freshman class. Manny did not feel it was necessary to validate his ethnicity by becoming a member of a formal student organization. He sounded skeptical of the influence of those organizations (the majority were sponsored by non-members of cultural groups) on Latino students' self-esteem and pride. When asked if he got involved in the Mexican American Chicano Association (MECHA) at school, he replied:

> At school you see more the African American club or the Native American club. All that is more for show than anything substantial. That's just bull_____ to me. We're all people made of the same things. You don't need a club to feel we're Mexican. We're proud, that comes from inside of you. You don't need a club to feel that.

Stereotyping: "Either Being Black or Mexican, You Are a Troublemaker or a Drug Dealer"

Manny was equally emphatic when he voiced his feelings about "White" psychology, behavior, and attitudes. The White adults at school appeared to ignore his academic potential, skills, and abilities. They convinced him, through looks and glances, that they viewed him as a dangerous influence and destined for academic failure. When I asked him how could he tell he was being stereotyped in this way, he answered:

> You can just feel it, the way a person looks at you, eye contact. The way they act. It's already made up in their minds. By their first two sentences you can already tell what they think of you. They would always be observing me, they would always take away my pager. My mom got it for me. I worked as a D.J. so they thought I was a drug dealer. I was tired of being stopped and harassed.

For Manny, the school's emphasis on controlling and expelling youths considered disobedient or dangerous, and the seeming acceptance that ethnicity or its symbols were automatic indicators of affiliation with a problematic group, communicated the idea that Latinos were troublemakers and irredeemable. Manny saw numerous Latinos drop out of school because they were perceived as troublemakers. As he described before, no Mexican-descent individuals were presented as role models. The few classes that attempted to address Latino issues were quickly dismantled. Manny explained:

> If I went through a whole day of teachers and administrators giving me nothing but grief and attitudes for the way I dress, speak, or look, I would drop out and leave too. I would say: "This school is bull_____ for me." I can go out and make money; I don't need school.

Manny said that the school authorities were always after him and waiting for an opportunity to expel him. The numerous incidents with the school's administration and its disciplinary measures forced Manny's parents to get involved and write letters to the district's superintendent. Manny explained:

> The assistant principal hated me 'cause my mom would always be there to back me up. Both my mom and dad would always be there. My mom would stop calling the school; she contacted the superintendent.

Consequently, school authorities could not expel Manny.

The frequent stigmatization of Manny at school because he drove nice vehicles, used a pager, defied authority, and rejected school rules landed him on a few occasions into more serious situations:

> They would never want to give me back my pager. There were these two times, they got a police officer to search me in front of my friends. They thought I was passing drugs because they would see me shaking hands with friends. I remember the cop at the office and the assistant principal. They would never say "I'm sorry" after they'd done their search.

After these incidents, Manny recalled that for a time he lost interest in school. He performed the minimum necessary to pass his classes and to please his parents.

> One day I got so tired of their suspicious attitudes, I said to myself, "OK, you think I'm a drug dealer? That's the image I am going to give you, but I'm graduating. How many drug dealers graduate?"

Manny explained that after a while the harassment and his "marked" identification of his being a troublemaker at school became an everyday situation to which he eventually grew accustomed:

> They always had it in for me and my friends. Ms. Cornwell, Mr. Pinfeld, and all of them. They hated us. They had memorized our matriculation numbers, last names, everything, they knew us that well, the monitors. We were *traviesos* [playful].

Manny was well aware that stereotyping and ethnic politics transcended school walls. He also was well aware of the role of power in our society and the influence that the media and television exert on people's attitudes. In the following quote, Manny shared his views on the south side of the city, the place where he resides:

> It's like the people on the media, how the media makes it sound when there's an incident on the southside. On TV they inform what happened and that's it. They don't dig deep into the problem. They make the southside look worse than it is. The southside ain't bad. There's just some people involved in bad things.

Manny's remarks indicate a good understanding of the local problems of his school and the community and its embeddedness in a world of power, politics, and economic injustice. He said:

> The southside is not that bad just because we don't have big houses, mansions, or make a bunch of money. Ain't no difference. Still we are people just like the people that live in mansions. Here you have low income or no income. You have to make ends meet. It boils down to economics again, to the economics in the world. The way this world runs. Schools are just like the Constitution. They were made for White people, the rich land-owning Anglo people that control the economy in the country.

Manny had never heard of Paolo Freire; nevertheless, his knowledge of complex economic forms of oppression reflects his awareness of the broader issues that impact schools. The issue of power to which Manny referred guided our discussion about power at both local and school levels. For

Manny, one the biggest problems with schools lies in the relationship between students and teachers.

Teachers: "The Straightforward Ones Versus the Bull_____rs"

For Manny good teachers gave students choices by asking them what and how they wanted to learn without imposing or exerting their power:

> Good teachers gave us choices; they did not show their power and control even if you chose not to do the work. They will still say "hi" to you when you see you in the hall. They will still be friendly; they were a person. But with other teachers if you were not making the grade, they wouldn't even look at you; you were just a matriculation number.

I asked Manny to expand what he meant by "gave us choices":

> Good teachers ask, "How do you want to learn? getting into groups, taking notes, research in the library, let's vote." They don't impose and control. I think we learn a lot better that way.

Manny recalled five "good teachers" during his entire school life:

> They were down to earth. They didn't try to bull_____ you. They just told you straight about what they wanted, what they expected, and that was it. People that make their classes interesting and funny. Earn their salaries the right way.

For Manny, teachers' attitudes were key to the students' determination to remain or leave school.

> I mean, I'm talking about being a person, being friendly. I think if more teachers were like that, more students would like to go to school. It's attitude. It's all it is. I mean, students have certain attitudes too, but if you show them that you care and you respect them. I still talk and keep phone numbers of the teachers I respect.

Good teachers for Manny were those who took your input as important, those who showed you respect, those who advocated and served as a voice for their students, even if it meant defying the system and its administration. He was emphatic when he said a caring teacher has a lot to do with students not only staying in school but also enjoying school. Manny explained:

> The teacher of my advance media class, he's a nice teacher, he treats you like a person, your "say" is important, your input is important. If you're a kid, oh well.

But your input is important. You get a good feeling from being respected. Teachers that are for the kids, more for our rights and for what we wanted to do. If we get one teacher, two teachers there voicing our opinions, and the way we feel, imagine how much better any school would be. Like again, my teacher, Mr. Sanchez, Ms. Cox [the assistant principal] hated him. Why? Because he was a teacher for us, he wanted school to be more for us.

I asked Manny how he knew that the school administration disliked Mr. Sanchez. Manny continued:

He would tell us everything that went on in school, even the stuff at the teachers' meetings. What you guys discuss in meetings. When something wrong happened in school, they would always blame Mr. Sanchez. He was a teacher for the students, he showed us his trust. He would tell us, "Don't be doing that, you got me in trouble, you little s_____." He would cuss. He was young like us.

Care, friendship, reducing the generation gap, and establishing and maintaining a relationship beyond the subject matter were also for Manny some of the characteristics of a good teacher. He found these characteristics in most of his Mexican-American teachers and role models:

Teachers should be more than teachers, but also friends. Like my graphics arts teacher, Mr. Sanchez, he would talk to us like if he was one more of the guys.

"Straightforward" teachers trust their students and treat them as adults, according to Manny:

I give you an example: If you miss the class with no excuse, good teachers treat you as adults without making a fuss, being nasty, or questioning. It's your choice, like in college. If you're treated like adults, you respond more. In college you could go to the bathroom anytime you wanted, not sit there in class and wait for hours till you get permission like in high school.

In contrast, Manny defined the "bull_____r" as the teacher who does not have the ability or the patience necessary to present his material in a variety of ways. As Manny put it, "They just want you to memorize their stuff." The "bull_____r's" only resource, Manny claimed, was to pick on students and embarrass them in front of the class so as to appear funny. Manny described frequent scenarios:

They spend long hours just talking. They are too concentrated in themselves; they don't even know or don't care if we are following or not. They explain things in ways we don't understand. If you ask them to repeat, they'd say: "Oh well, pay attention." They'd embarrass you with a remark or others would say, "Read the book if you didn't get it."

Teachers make comments on the way you dress, they embarrass students, and make the class laugh at the expense of students. An English teacher once made a joke about me and my looks. I answer back, and said something about his wife. He didn't like that. He got serious and said, "All right, that's enough." They don't like when you fire back.

According to Manny, bad teachers concentrated excessively on enforcing discipline and used and abused their power through referrals. He narrated several incidents that resulted in his transferring out of classes. The following is one such critical incident:

You have two choices: follow their rules or leave the class. I had a teacher; he was the media/communication teacher. He got up furiously, and yelled at me just because I got up and threw a piece of trash away. "You didn't ask permission to get up from your seat" in front of the whole class. I thought to myself: All these teachers, adults. I wonder why we act like kids, because we get treated like kids. That was elementary school stuff. That was not for people our age. I left the class and went to see my counselor to transfer out of that class. He followed me down the hall yelling and handing me a referral. He threw a big fit just because I stood up to throw a piece of paper. I knew I was not going to get along with him. Those are the teachers with a big power trip.

Manny regretted not having had an audio or video recorder to record the incidents that illustrated the power relations and numerous teacher–student incidents he observed in school:

I just wish in any of those days, I could have taken a camera or something, and show you how school really is. You could see exactly how things happen. What really goes on inside the school. What language the people who run the school use. That's probably why they didn't want us to record in media classes. They'd take cameras away from us.

Administration and School Policy: "It's That Little Power Trip Again"

Manny's awareness and sensitivity to the role of a school administrator, who can empower students or culturally isolate students, can be seen in his evaluation of the activities during school lunch hour. Manny appeared highly attuned to the degree of emotional support that administrators did or did not provide and to the ways in which they used their power and handled relationships with students. During our interviews, Manny frequently made reference to the school principal during his freshman year and compared him to the administrator who replaced him during the rest of his high school career. As stated previously, Manny's first principal in high school was suddenly removed from his position for failing to raise low standardized test scores. Mr. Gatelo, a Mexican American raised in the community, was a principal who "knew all the school's students by their first name." According to Manny, the new principal, an African-American female, did not hide her favoritism toward the 5% African-American students in the school. She became the sponsor of an ethnic student club and, he said, promoted racial confrontations with the larger Latino student body. According to Manny, she was just "the principal for the Blacks":

> She protected only the Blacks. You would always see her with Black kids even when the school was 85% Hispanic. I'd always see her with Black kids. I never saw her talking to Mexican kids, really even caring. The old principal, Mr. Gatelo, *that* was a principal. I was a freshman then. At lunch, he would walk around table to table seeing how you were doing. "What's going on?" he would tell us, just talking to you. He would greet everybody by their first name, everybody, everybody. This principal, all I've seen her doing was to sit by her little perch everyday at lunch just watching us. Just watching us. There were fights, and she wouldn't even see.

Manny's account suggests the complex and insidious ways in which school administrators and the structure of the school itself can both reflect and promote racist attitudes. For Manny, those attitudes were revealed in an administration that did not make any effort to reach students or to interact with them. The great cultural distance that Latino students felt with their principal is revealed in Manny's following statement:

> One thing I know is that we really didn't care for Ms. Robertson. Seriously, when we were graduating, in the auditorium, an assistant principal came on the microphone to announce that the principal was not coming for the ceremony. I mean everybody stood up and cheered. Everyone cheered loud—I mean I stood up and cheered loud with them too. The whole graduating class cheered her not coming.

Several times during our interviews Manny complained about the lengthy bureaucratic procedures to resolve problems in his school. In his view, all the punitive programs at school did not resolve anything but held the students further behind academically. Programs such as tardy policies, "lockout," in-school suspensions, or suspensions that prevented students from going to school anywhere from 10 to 21 or more days impeded students from attending classes. Manny explained, "It is almost impossible for students to catch up on the large amount of missed assignments." Manny viewed these negative discipline programs as "dropout reproducers":

When they'd call me to the office to get a tardy or discipline detention I was always missing all the classes. I remember waiting in the office for hours to be seen. There were 5 assistant principals, I don't know what they were doing but they were never available. I used to miss 3 whole class periods just waiting for them in the office. Great waste of time. Then, they wonder why there are so many dropouts. You miss a lot of schooling that way.

Manny commented about the school's tardy policies in this way:

Lockout was another big joke too. Sometimes my girlfriend and I would get to school late. I had to go pick her up in the morning and you know how girls are. They'd send us to a room for being late, and they'd make you stand throughout the whole period. Physically standing out for a long period. You got tired. One day I was ready to pass out. But the point is, what a waste of time. They didn't teach me nothing. Lockout should be more like a time to do homework, or read, do something more productive than just standing there. They treated us like in a prison. I used to mouth off, complain, and tell them what I thought but they would give me more detention. After a while I preferred to stay in-school suspension until 12:00 every day. That's why I used to hate school.

Manny's frustrations were evident when I asked him what solutions he would implement if he were a school administrator:

I'd find a better way if I want that students stay in school. Make them come on Saturday morning or real early. Make them come like they did at the "Breakfast Club." Have you seen that movie? I think a lot more people would be there on time. But I mean, even adults are tardy. You are not perfect. I've seen teachers late; they can't even do it and they expect us to do it.

One other administrative aspect that Manny found unnecessary and out of place was that of the principal's excessive display of power. The daily confrontations in Manny's school among monitors, administrators, and students very often resulted in physically violent acts. The school authorities speaking through radios resulted in an environment that looked more like a prison than an educational institution. Manny believed that the school personnel at times took their jobs too far:

It comes into that little power trip again. The principals, they would try to do their job too far, too good. One time when a monitor asked me to show him my ID, he started pushing me. I pushed him back. This was all the time. The monitors would chase you, run after you—that's not their job. Their job is to inform the principals if you do something wrong. But they would get in a fight with you. There were so many times I would have swung at monitors but then who are the principals going to believe? So what could you do? They don't respect you there.

Dropouts: ". . . But I Know How to Play the Game"

Finally, Manny and I talked about the students who drop out, for example, the half a million Latinos who did not graduate in 1995. Manny was almost one of them, but his parents were there for him in the difficult times. Manny thought dropouts lacked the patience to put up with the system and its administration. He felt that the school was not the real world and that part of the problem lies in the fact that students are treated like children who are not trusted:

> My friends who dropped out didn't put in their heads that a bit of patience is necessary to put up with those people. Understand that they are full of s_____ and that you just have to cope with that for 4 years. They'd be writing referrals, and I'd be thinking, "These people are full of s_____. This ain't the real world." They want to teach us about the real world, and here they are treating us like kids. I think dropouts take it too seriously.

In addition to his strong criticism of the school administration and policies, he also mentioned the responsibility that teachers have in the increasing problem of students' academic disengagement. Some teachers, he added, damage the self-esteem of students when they stereotype and doubt their academic capability. After Manny graduated, he was employed at a car-stereo store where he is now the main manager and he enrolled in some courses at a local community college. In the future, he hopes to own his own business.

Conclusion

"Pursuit of the American dream" is one of the dominant themes in Manny's view of the world. He viewed stereotypes about Latinos, the advantages that Anglos have in society, a school curriculum designed for Whites, and the power struggle among teachers and students as all potentially working against enjoying his own version of the American dream. Throughout his schooling, Manny saw three ways to achieve the dream: by "playing the game" (a strategy counseled by his parents); through drugs and crime (the choice of some of his peers who have "succeeded); or through entrepreneurship and self-employment. He tended to favor the third alternative as the fastest, least risky, and practical path toward attainment of the dream. His negative experiences at school, the power struggle that represented gaining respect from teachers and validating his identity, along with the uncertainty of still being unemployed after obtaining a higher degree, all discouraged him from continuing his education. Nevertheless, Manny does not rule out the possibility of taking college classes in the near future to enhance his knowledge of mechanics and electronics.

In retrospect, Manny viewed school as a "big problem" in which societal power relationships are played out between dominants and subordinates. In school he saw all the dynamics of the society at large. In school, however, those dynamics were enacted by the administrators and teachers against the students. Manny identified a variety of coping strategies that helped him survive school, although he often defied the system with his parents' backing. Manny viewed school as being oppressive and "a big waste of time." It did not represent the "real world." Students dropped out, he believed, because they could not tolerate the constant stereotyping and lack of connection to real life. They felt no connection between school and community, its problems or its assets. Hence, "playing the game" wastes time in terms of gaining practical skills and experience needed to get a job and succeed in the real world. Manny viewed school as not being connected to the real world, observing that some subject matter, such as science, provided little room to exercise imagination or to learn in a way that is satisfying, participatory, and relevant. Manny complained much about lack of relevance of curriculum and even asked, "Why study about a bunch of White guys? What have they ever done for us?" A single Mexican literature class was one ray of hope and a positive experience in Manny's high school experience.

Manny referred to most of his high school teachers as "bull_____rs" whose only skills were to exercise power and enforce strict discipline. He said these teachers were not sympathetic to students' needs. At the opposite end of the spectrum were the "straightforward teachers" who advocated for and were friends to the students. These teachers were in the minority and, for the most part, were Latinos.

In terms of identity, Manny left his high school experience feeling he had "proven them wrong" in terms of the stereotyped images his teachers and administrators had of him. His view of himself as both a Mexican American and a Latino is typical of those who have been forced to leave their culture and language behind in order to assimilate. Manny stated, "I don't fit in over here, and I don't fit over there," suggesting that communication and Spanish language ability seem to be the main barriers between him and Mexican immigrants. However, his allegiance to his ancestry and heritage and the importance he gave to his family were evident. As he stated, he stayed in school mainly to please his parents. He did not perceive cultural or ideological differences between himself and recent Mexican immigrants: "My family just came first." His statement made reference to the cultural and ideological parallels he perceived between recent immigrants and American-born Mexican Americans. Even with other minority groups he seemed to find parallel worldviews. Manny maintained that "a superiority feeling" created the greatest distance between him and Whites. For Manny, there was a clear distinction between the "haves" and the "have nots," the powerful and the powerless, and the Whites and all other groups.

He saw pursuing a career as an "iffy" proposition because it would not guarantee a good job or a piece of the American dream. He valued time and felt that high school should be a two-year endeavor in which all students should have the chance to begin a college major early. He felt that school had deprived him of time to learn a good skill with which to support himself and had deprived him of other opportunities he could have enjoyed to achieve the dream. Manny "survived" school to please his parents and to bolster his own pride in spite of the stereotypes and racism he encountered.

FOR DISCUSSION

1. Teachers' views about "success," according to Manny, are restricted to being admitted to a university and receiving a college degree. As educators, how do we communicate to our students that we respect each person's definition of success? What is your definition of success? Do your cultural values influence your definition?

2. Manny's statement, "I don't fit in over here, and I don't fit over there," reveals his ambivalence in defining his cultural identity. If you were Manny's teacher, how would you assist him in dealing with his feelings?

3. Manny states that in his school (where 65% of the student population were Latinos) history was studied only from the White man's perspective. As an educator at Manny's school, what steps would you take to restructure the curriculum and to ensure that all cultural perspectives represented at the school were heard and included? What rationale would you present to your principal to implement changes?

4. What does Manny really mean when he says that "school is a mechanical game and a waste of time." Provide specific examples of ways in which the school promotes these feelings?

5. Manny had a series of disciplinary incidents with the school authorities. His parents stated that they were only called by the school when the situation had deteriorated. What are some ways in which schools could work together with parents to prevent misunderstandings and disciplinary actions from happening?

6. The messages that adults send to adolescents can have a great effect on them and eventually create a self-fulfilling prophecy. What are the messages that Manny's school sent to him? How do labels relate to self-fulfilling prophecy? Can you give examples from your own experience?

7. Standing for hours facing a wall was one of the punishments Manny received at school for being late. Can you explain the difference between a consequence and a punishment? Does discipline mean punishment? What are some problems

with using punishment to teach? Have you ever experienced any of these problems yourself?

8. One of the only classes Manny enjoyed in high school was his Southwestern literature class taught by a Mexican-American educator who knew how to present Manny's culture in a positive way. Unfortunately, the principal removed the course from the school's curriculum and this teacher was given a different assignment. Manny's negative feelings about schooling increased at this point. What do you think about trying to match teachers to students' cultural and language background? Explain the benefits.

9. According to Manny, the principal at his school favored students of her own ethnicity. She was the sponsor of an ethnic club and she frequently took students on out-of-state trips to attend national conferences. She also closely monitored their academic progress, which rapidly placed these students in honor academic lists. What do you think is the message that this administrator was giving to the remaining 65% Latino student body at the school?

10. A group of teachers and you have been asked to determine why a particular Latino student has been doing poorly in your class. What are the aspects that you decide to look at?

4 Introducing Carla: "This Is America and Here You Speak English!"

I met Carla in 1989 when she was a freshman at a rural high school in southern Arizona. I had been hired to run the English as a Second Language and the French departments. The school administration had made it clear that they were more interested in developing the French foreign language program than in investing in a bilingual program for the increasing numbers of Latino students. Our deep philosophical differences on this point eventually drove me to resign and to accept a new high school teaching position in an urban high school.

That fall, as I was looking for ideal candidates for my study at my new urban secondary site, a high school counselor handed me a list of three possible students. These high school Latinos indeed embodied the characteristics I needed for my study. Such characteristics included students who were at risk for abandoning their education or facing problems with schools' disciplinary policies and practices. One of the students in the list was Carla. Destiny had reunited us again. I recognized Carla's bright smile as she entered my office. When I last saw her, she was a young freshman. Now she was a mature senior. She told me she had dropped out of the rural school in the middle of her junior year because of a conflict with the school principal. She had stayed home for two years because there were no other high schools nearby the rural community where she lived. She had left her parents' home to live in the city with an aunt who had encouraged her to finish school.

Carla was now enrolled at Mountain High School, a school that had the largest Latino population in the city and a student body that exceeded 2,000 students. Entering an urban high school was a big transition for Carla who was accustomed to a small rural conservative high school in which diversity was not too visible. Carla's graduation was again at risk because of a conflict with her senior English teacher. This time, however, Carla had the support of her counselor, the bilingual education coordinator, and even the Mexican-American principal who was investigating her grade complaint. It appeared that there had been complaints against this ESL teacher in the past.

One of today's Latina adolescents.

I asked Carla to give me news about the rural school where we had met in 1989. She told me that most of her Mexican peers had also dropped out for a variety of reasons. "The school's bilingual program was dismantled, and the few teachers who helped us, Mexicans, had been fired or just left," she said. Carla had turned into a very attractive young woman. Added to her physical attributes, her pleasant personality and sense of humor permitted her to gain friends everywhere. She was very popular at Mountain High not only among her friends but also among administrators and bilingual teachers alike.

Carla exhibited a sense of confidence and a self-assurance that were products of personal growth and mental maturity. The two years spent at home after she dropped out had made her reflect a lot, she related. At the end of our first encounter she stated very convincingly, "This time I will not let anybody stand in my way."

She viewed education as the most direct path to desirable material and behavioral benefits but especially as a way to fulfill her ideal of helping others. Her immediate goals were clear: graduate, attend the local community college, and eventually become a bilingual teacher. During our first encounter, she said something that intrigued me: "I want to teach the children all the things they haven't taught me." I knew then that I wanted to learn more about her schooling experience and about the things she claimed that teachers had not taught her. I realized that given the obstacles she had faced in the past and the new ones she was experiencing during her senior year, Carla was the ideal candidate for my study.

She gracefully agreed to be interviewed with the condition that all our interviews be conducted in Spanish. I understood that using her native language would be more relaxing for her to narrate her schooling experiences. Our sessions were recorded and transcribed in Spanish, but in writing this chapter I translated all direct quotes into English. We thought that this would facilitate the management and readability of the enormous body of data.

Carla's drive to *llegar a ser alguien* (become someone) originated from trying to prove to herself that she could accomplish her goals. She also wanted to prove her parents wrong. They had always doubted that Carla had any academic aspirations. "My parents compared me with my little sister who would always get good grades." They thought I could never take school seriously, she complained. When Carla dropped out of school, her parents were resigned to accept that their daughter would get married and raise children like so many other Latina girls. Observing her determination, her parents finally granted her permission to move to the city to live with her aunt and finish her high school education.

Carla was raised in a family committed to vigorous adaptation and change. Carla's large family, separated by the United States–Mexican border, is representative of many other Mexican families in the United States. Through many generations, Carla's relatives inhabited both sides of the border town of Nogales, Arizona. Carla's father was born and raised in Bacobampo, a small agricultural town near Obregon-Sonora that was severely affected by the Mexican economic downturn. Her father became a seasonal worker in the United States until the early 1980s. When pressed by the severe Mexican economic crisis, in 1988 he petitioned to migrate permanently with his wife and three children to the United States. Carla's father secured the family's financial situation through his hard-working nature and good manual skills. He remodeled houses for a contractor's firm in Arizona.

Carla was 12 years old when she crossed the Mexican border to join her father in Phoenix. The transition was a difficult and abrupt experience for her. She left behind not only a familiar culture and language but also the peaceful rural lifestyle she was accustomed to in Mexico. She vividly recalled the affluent public middle school near Phoenix she attended upon her arrival. She recalled the modern audio-visual support and individualized instruction she received while learning her first English words. The technological support and the good instruction, she said, helped her make enormous progress in English. She regretted that because of her father's work the family had to move to southern Arizona six months later. She explained:

At the school I was in Phoenix I learned a lot. It was the best school I've ever been in. They would use all kinds of machines, projectors, and they would give me earphones. I would listen to the lessons explained in two languages, Spanish and English. There were very few Mexicans though. I liked it there, too bad we had to move down here.

Carla finished her middle school in a small rural school district. The district was primarily funded by property taxes paid by a nearby affluent, conservative, retirement community. In addition to large ranches and a pecan factory, the community had several small Mormon churches. Senior community members played a vital role in the decision making and functions of the schools. The district consisted of three schools: an elementary school, a middle school, and a high school. The student and staff populations were very homogeneous. The high school, for example, did not have any African-American or Native-American students or staff members. In the early 1990s, however, a large influx of Mexican immigrants changed the community's make-up. Among them were Carla, her older brother, and a younger sister. The district, as seen through Carla's testimony, was not prepared for this influx.

"I Didn't Like Their Pushy Ways"

Language and *English* were the most frequently used words in all my interviews with Carla. She was especially sensitive to the word *language*. For her, the issue of language was delicate and critical. She realized that English was necessary if you wanted to succeed in this country, but she firmly believed that it should not be acquired at the expense of her own language. During more than a decade of residence in the United States, Carla's parents conducted all their daily activities and transactions in Spanish. In the rural community where they lived (an hour away from the Mexican border), there were no adult evening English as a Second Language courses they could attend. Like her parents, Carla maintained a strong emotional commitment to her Mexican and immigrant identity through her mother tongue. Carla's adherence to the language as a marker of her identity, which she did not want to give up, was perceived by Carla's teachers and school administrators as rebelling against assimilation. Because of this language "battle," Carla and her brothers gained a reputation that eventually resulted in their dropping out of school.

Carla manifested her oppositional identity through language and resisted pressures to bow to a dominant culture. The dilemma between the pressure of conforming to the rules versus remaining loyal to her language and culture is revealed in the following excerpt:

> I didn't like to speak English. Teachers would call my parents to school to tell them that I didn't want to speak English. They would say things like, "This is America and English is spoken here!" I didn't like their pushy ways. They wanted me to speak in English even during lunch. I would speak it with people that did not know me. I can speak good English, but these were teachers that spoke Spanish. I didn't need to speak it with them.

The language pressure came from all corners. According to Carla, Anglo and Latino teachers alike would use their power to demand total assimilation.

Her frustration was evident when she voiced her concern that there was unequal status between the Spanish and the English language speakers. She also demonstrated her resistance by suggesting that her acquaintances make some effort to cross into her social world:

> The Mexican teachers were the worst. I remember Mr. Moreno, he was a racist, but there were a few Anglos too. They wanted me to greet them in English every day. The more they demanded, the least I would speak in English. I know that this is America, but I think Americans should also speak Spanish. I wonder what they'd feel if they were forced to speak it. Sometimes there is too much pressure.

I asked her to tell me more about Mr. Moreno and why she defined him as a racist. She explained:

> You could tell by the way he treated you and talked to you. He couldn't look more Mexican, but he was the most racist of all. When I was a freshman, they'd give me after-school detention for arriving late or for not speaking English. One day, I was 5 minutes late and was sent to after-school detention. Mr. Moreno was in charge of detention that day. He'd tell me, "Speak in English or I will not let you go home this afternoon." I wouldn't do it and we stayed until after 6:00 p.m. My parents were so worried.

Carla revealed that when students experience an environment that is not coercive and unfriendly, but collaborative and nurturing, students respond and enjoy school:

> When I saw a teacher or a gringo friend making an attempt to speak to me in Spanish, I would speak to them in English. It is nice to see they're trying to understand you. But my freshman teachers when they had meetings, they would all talk about the students that did not speak English and they'd give us bad grades because of that. They were very demanding.

"All of Us Mexicans Got Fs"

Since Carla had experienced high school in both urban and rural environments, I asked her to list some differences between the two settings. In particular, I was interested in her perceptions about the situations that constrain or enable Latino students' motivation at school in both rural and urban environments. Carla's first statements had to do with racial conflicts and stereotyping. In Carla's worldview, the degree to which students let these societal problems affect them will either discourage or empower them to continue struggling toward graduation. During her first years in high school at the rural school, Carla did not conform to assimilationist or stereotypical pressures, which resulted in her dropping out. Her silent and shy self was the product of her English language insecurities and of her location in a social system in which she and her peers were viewed and treated as inferior. The post-dropout Carla gained a sense of assertiveness and a determination. This oppositional-self was able to ignore discriminatory practices and develop strategies to succeed. Carla said:

> I think there are more dropouts in urban schools first because there are more students; there are fights between students of different races. You can also see teachers or administrators that prefer certain students and reject others. In my experience, you can find more people to help you too. In the urban school, at Mountain High, I found bilingual teachers who helped me a lot. In the rural school because we Mexicans were just a small group, there were bad teachers who openly offended you, insulted you, or were openly racist.

I asked her to give me specific examples of those she believed were racists. In addition to Mr. Moreno, she mentioned two teachers during her freshman days at her rural school, a physical education teacher whose name was Ms. Cueva and her American history teacher whose name was Mr. Eliado. Coincidentally, these two educators were also of Mexican descent. She explained:

> My friends had warned me not to take a class with Ms. Cueva, but to take it from the other P. E. teacher, a gringo. He was nice but I didn't listen to them. In that class, we had to run one mile every day. If a Mexican did not run it or complete the mile she'd immediately give you an F, but if a gringo did not run it and give her an excuse she'd say, "Ok, that's fine." She wouldn't trust us. What a strange coincidence that all the Mexicans had F's in the semester or in the quarter. Only if one day you didn't run, we'd get an F.

I asked her if she had spoken to a counselor or the school principal about this teacher's attitude. Carla's point of view was that minority students had little ability to affect change or to be heard. She replied, "It was of no use, the principal was just like her; he wouldn't believe us." Consequently, Carla retained a negative orientation toward school as new interactions with teachers would confirm her feeling that "Mexicans were not wanted."

"I'm Not a Wetback!"

In several interviews Carla primarily talked about what she considered her worst experience during her initial high school year. Carla and her school friends used to avoid going to their history class by hiding in the girls' bathroom. Mr. Eliado, a veteran Mexican-American teacher, enjoyed joking around at the expense of his students. But according to Carla, Mexican students were the only ones picked as subjects of his nasty sense of humor. Mexican students who were sensitive about their legal status and language skills would take Mr.

Eliado's jokes as direct invitations to leave the school. According to Carla, many students dropped out of school as a result of negative exchanges with this teacher and his offensive remarks. She described the situation:

> My friends and I used to run out the door as soon as the dismissal bell would ring to avoid his picking on us. There were a couple of times we cried. He was mean. . . . He would pick on the shy students, the ones that couldn't respond to him in English. Before the beginning of the class he'd yell across the patio, "Wetbacks! *La migra* is coming to get you!" Or . . . "I saw you the other day jumping over the border fence. How did you do it? Did you hurt yourself? Did you cut your hands?" He would yell so loud across the patio that other teachers would hear. He would embarrass us in front of everybody.

I noticed how Carla vividly remembered all details of these encounters. For Carla, it was very important to distinguish between immigrants who crossed the border illegally and those who made it with the proper documentation. In her opinion, she could not be considered a "wetback" because she had entered the United States legally and as a result of her father's petition. Mr. Eliado "insulted you simply because you spoke Spanish," she explained. Since he was the only history teacher, Anglo students were also placed in his classes. Carla remembers being ashamed in front of her Anglo peers:

> He'd be explaining a lesson and he'd call your name. He'd say it in both languages to make sure everyone understood it and he would distort the sounds in our names. I was embarrassed a few times in front of all the class. The gringos would laugh at us. He wouldn't pick on the gringos though. He knew they'd respond to him. Sometimes what he'd say was so strong that we'd feel like crying or strangling him. But we'd hide it and pretend we were enjoying his jokes. That way he'd leave us alone. There were times when the principal would walk in, but he'd continue with his jokes and even the principal would celebrate them.

Consequently, Carla and her Mexican peers felt as outsiders in an environment in which language was a huge social and educational barrier.

Carla spoke in great detail about several teachers, many of them of Mexican descent, whom she perceived as racist. The average person equates racism with the activity of the Ku Klux Klan or the neo-Nazis who direct acts of violence against people of color. We do not realize that this spiritual illness manifests itself in more subtle ways, in the form of attitudes that trigger behaviors we deem natural and justifiable. It has not been unusual for me (not only through the testimonies of Carla and Manny but during my 12 years in public schools in Arizona) to hear students complain about the attitudes and subconscious air of superiority that educated professionals display against Mexican immigrants and other bicultural students. Racism and prejudice transcend ethnic background and skin color. Many American-born Mexican

Americans as well as Black educators often teach the way they learned, replicating much of their earlier experiences, pain, and frustration in their own classrooms. As Rutstein (1993) stated, "The civil rights of the sixties was able to eliminate some of the effects of racism, but failed to eradicate the cause" (p. 8). The creation of multicultural programs and enforcement of affirmative action projects in almost all schools in the nation have not done away with this problem. In many cases, school districts implement superficial programs just to show the public that they honor diversity and that something is being done to reduce racism and prejudice. Within every ethnic group there are men and women who claim being politically progressive, yet their actions reflect harmful prejudices they may not be conscious of. It is the role of the school to be more in tune with students' points of view in order to create nurturing environments in which educators and students can speak freely about these issues.

My interviews with Carla continued. I wanted to know about the specific incident that resulted in her dropping out of this rural school in the middle of her junior year.

"Only Mexicans Drop Out"

Carla recalled that her decision to drop out was not a result of one single incident but of a series of negative situations that created an unbearable environment for her:

> Too many things came together the same time I came to the conclusion that there was too much racism in that school. What a coincidence that only Mexicans would drop out.

Besides the language pressures and Mr. Eliados' classes, she mentioned other institutional roadblocks, such as "strict school policies," which she found impeded her smooth integration into an American educational setting. In particular, she recalled the school's tardy policies, rooted in cultural idiosyncrasies, which caused her to have confrontations with school authorities. It was because of a tardy infraction that Carla was sent to see the school principal. After an especially negative interaction with him, she decided to drop out of school. Most Latino students do not consider being late to class merits a serious reprimand. Carla's older brother had dropped out of school in his senior year because of his frequent visits to the principal's office: "My brother got bored with so many rules. They chased him away." Because Carla's family lived in a ranch area about 45 minutes away from the school, they had problems getting to school on time. In regards to the critical incident with the school principal, Carla described the following event:

The principal had to sign my tardy referral so I went to his office. It was the first time I went with a referral to his office, but he talked to me like if he were tired of seeing me there. He said, "Aren't you Raul's sister? You are just like your brother, always getting in trouble. Why don't you go home? You are not interested in school."

Carla said that the principal's strong words left her speechless. She was skeptical that her tardy infraction was the real reason for the principal's anger. He warned her that after one more tardiness he would suspend her from school and advised Carla to bring her parents to school. She took the strong encounter with the principal as a direct invitation to leave the school and instead of telling her parents what had really happened, she told them that she had been expelled for being late to school:

I knew that the principal was going to be on my case and I didn't want to give him the pleasure to chase me away one day. I told my parents, I had been expelled for being late. It hurt me because I only needed three more months to finish my junior year. I didn't want all the school to know I had been expelled. I preferred to voluntarily leave.

Carla's parents manifested an immigrant's reaction to conformism and powerlessness. In part, due to their limited English proficiency, they chose not to confront the principal over the incident with Carla:

My father wanted to go to see the principal but he decided against it. After all, the principal was an Anglo and he was a Mexican. If the principal told me all those terrible things in his office, can you imagine what he'd tell my parents? Maybe "Why don't you go back to Mexico" or something like that. My father couldn't go to complain because he doesn't speak English—neither does my mother.

Carla and her friends also had trouble understanding other school rules. There were times when some of her friends were sent to the office for talking or trying to help each other with school work. As she explained, class organization differed greatly from what she was used to in Mexican schools. Her Mexican classes were organized around the concept of cooperation and peer tutoring. Students helped one another, talked in class, and shared, she explained. Carla learned that in the United States the orientation is more individualistic. She explained:

They would send you to the office for any little thing. There were too many rules in that school. They watch you all the time. You have to inform them everything you were doing. Sometimes my friends would get referrals for trying to help me understand the homework. We'd talk in Spanish. The teachers thought we were talking about them, or laughing about them, and they'd write referrals and send you to the office.

Carla's statements reveal that the schools focused on direct forms of social control, including close surveillance and constraining students' movements. The data Carla provided suggest that although this type of administration succeeded in reducing deviant activities, in the long run it had its drawbacks. Severe disciplinary measures inhibited the integration of students into school. The large numbers of Latinos subjected to disciplinary actions, and the school environment itself, worked together to communicate the idea that Mexican students were disobedient and irredeemable.

Carla's gradual academic disengagement emerged as she began to notice patterns in the school environment that associated ethnicity with failure:

> We were always placed in classes where teachers were very strict with discipline. I remember Mr. Essert, our biology teacher, he'd yell all day long.

Carla began to realize that the school operated and acted with lower expectations for Latinos than for their Anglo counterparts. In her experience such expectations were communicated in three primary ways. First, teachers and administrators appeared to watch, show their fear, and keep their distance from Latino students, especially when they indicated allegiance to their culture and language. Second, instruction was not oriented and organized according to their learning style which included collaborative activities and social proximity. Third, although school officials and teachers demanded English as the sole medium of communication, Latino students were not provided with opportunities to interact with their Anglo peers to gain language competence. Carla's sense of cultural isolation is revealed in the following excerpt:

> In my fours years of high school, I can only remember two, at the most three, classes in which we studied with gringos. Most of the time we were just Mexicans. You see? I was always in ESL classes. I did not have any Anglo friends.

"My Extended Family"

Carla started school in the Mexican bordertown of Nogales. She remembered her school days and particularly her teachers whom she called "my second parents." In her opinion, the problem with the disproportionate number of dropouts in the United States has much to do with teachers who limit their role to that of a simple "instructor." Carla characterized these teachers as those who only lecture and leave the classroom quickly:

Here most of the teachers are always in a hurry. They only have time to make more money, not to talk to us. You enter your class, the teacher lectures and you are out. In Mexico, teachers worry. You feel they care about you. If they see you sad or inattentive after class they'd approach and ask, "What's wrong? Can I help?" Teachers there have time to be more human. I say that this has something to do with staying in school.

Carla seemed to suggest that the role of a teacher should not be only that of an instructor but also of a friend and confidante, especially in times when adolescents face great challenges in a rapidly deteriorating society. Carla described her Mexican teachers as her extended family. Being emotionally attached to their teachers who impart instruction with care and love, students feel obliged not to disappoint them:

Teachers there give you options and they do it with care and love. You feel like it'll be unfair to disappoint them. Here, there are only a few teachers that care and repeat to you importance of school. If you don't have a parent at home that pushes you to study and you don't have that person at school either, you do whatever you want. That is why many kids quit school. Finding a teacher that really cares for you is like finding a needle in the sand.

Carla attended the Pestalozzi public school in Nogales. Evaluating her experiences there, she stated that there were both negative and positive sides of Mexican schooling. Among the positive aspects she mentioned that teachers have a real "call for service." They have the patience to teach you until you learn. Most of the time, they did not start a new lesson until the previous lesson was mastered by everyone in the class:

My experience in Mexican schools was good and bad at the same time. Good because they teach very well there. They teach you until you learn even when sometimes we are 40 or 45 students in class, we wouldn't start a new lesson until everyone had learned. The bad part was that there were always a few slow learners and we had to wait until they got it. Our teachers were like our second parents. They had the right to reprimand us, punish us. Our parents gave them that authorization.

Carla then compared the teachers she had encountered in Mexican schools with those in the United States. Unfortunately for Carla, most teachers she encountered in American schools reaffirmed her oppositional identity and made her long for her old days in Nogales:

Here it's different. If you understood the lesson and the explanation, it's fine. But if you didn't, it's your problem. You are on your own. Teachers don't feel it is their obligation. In Mexico they try harder to help you, I think.

I asked Carla to expand on this theme:

> For example, I remember this teacher that made her lectures very difficult to un-
> derstand. In that class not even the best student would understand her expla-
> nation. It was a science class and a Mexican-American female teacher Ms.
> Rendon. We'd ask her to repeat the lesson, and she'd get mad and accused us of
> not paying attention. We'd go after school and she'd say she was too busy to see
> us. The whole class would fail her tests. Some teachers are too busy lecturing,
> talking to themselves at a different level, not at our level.

It occurred to me that Carla had had too many negative experiences with
Mexican-descent American teachers. I wanted to know if this was just a coin-
cidence or if she felt that Chicano teachers were not caring or supportive of
new Mexican immigrants:

> Unfortunately, in my experience, Chicano teachers were not that nice to me. But
> I know that not all are like that. In all my years in high school, I can remember
> at least two Latino teachers that were dedicated and caring. They liked to teach
> and to be with students. But they were soon replaced or they left the school.
> They were both immigrants themselves though. I remember Mr. Encinas, a
> sheltered-English teacher. He was nice and caring. He used to tell us stories
> about his first days in the United States without knowing English just like us. He
> used to tell us that we could become a teacher like him. He was only one year in
> the school and then he left. He didn't get along with the principal.

Carla's words reflected a sense that teachers who were caring and
student-centered and who acted as advocates for Mexican students were not
favored by school authorities. Carla summed up her feeling of powerlessness
when referring to the school principal: "He wanted to get rid of us one by one."
    On our initial interview and while I was explaining to Carla the nature
of my study, she mentioned her desire to become an elementary school teacher.
Her statement, "I want to teach children the things they haven't taught me"
had made an impression on me and I asked Carla to clarify further:

> What I meant is that there are things I learned in Mexico that you cannot learn
> here. This is a different world. Everybody now talks about computers. You have
> to study that. It's the career of the future. You can get more money. Everything
> is around money. People don't study what they like but what gives more money.
> I mean in Mexico sometimes it is like that too, but we also learn about little
> things. There are topics that can be insignificant but they teach you a lot. Teach-
> ers talk about life, about love, about sharing.

Not all of Carla's memories were negative. On several occasions
throughout our interviews she mentioned her school mentors. For Carla they
were crucial advocates who helped her negotiate and balance the multiple dimensions of her new cultural reality.

Mentors: "The Trick Is to Find Them"

Carla talked about the bilingual secretary at her rural high school who served as translator and interpreter between Mexican immigrant students and school authorities:

> Maria, the school secretary, she would help us translate school letters when we wouldn't understand English or she would give us advice about how to behave with certain teachers. She was very nice with us. They started accusing her of spending too much time with us. She began to have problems with the principal and one day we didn't see her anymore.

Another person Carla remembered with gratitude was the nurse's assistant who created an after-school student club to develop the artistic talents of Latino students. Yolanda, the nurse's assistant, wanted to reduce the cultural isolation of Latino students. She understood that what these students needed was to be proud of their talents and build up their self-esteem. Through expressing their skills, they would feel a sense of integration into the school's life. Carla explained that Yolanda sponsored a dance club in order to motivate Latinos to enjoy school and stay in it. Students who did not take part in sports or honors academic organizations and who experienced a sense of worthlessness soon found a place where their talents were valued. Carla belonged to such group, and for a long time the club kept her motivated and academically engaged. According to Carla, since the foundation of the club, student fights and other confrontations had ceased. Carla said:

> Many Mexican kids liked to fight but since she formed the club, the conflicts and fights stopped. We began to organize fund raisers and everybody would put the club first. Even at lunch time we would be rehearsing. It was difficult to find a room to practice. Mainly we heard Mexican music. Teachers wouldn't like to lend us their rooms. The principal would come to check us out, always suspecting about our activities.

The student club became a positive method of channeling students' energies. The dance club, which was also open to students other than Latinos, met several times a week during lunch hour and after school. Yolanda began fund raisers, arranged public presentations, and even accepted invitations to perform in a university event and at other high schools. The club soon became the largest student organization at school with over 80 members, but as the club gained popularity, the school's climate began to deteriorate. According to Carla, problems arose out of cultural misunderstandings between Anglo and Latino students. In view of the group's success, the school administration intervened in the club's activities and limited the organization's membership to students who maintained grades of C+ or better. These restrictions were perceived by the Latino students as coercive and biased because most of them were the ones receiving low grade-point averages. Then the Anglo students protested against the Spanish name given to the group and accused the group's sponsor of favoritism toward Mexicans. Carla continued:

> I remember that Yolanda started having problems with the principal and some teachers who were pushing her to put the grade restriction. The gringos accused her of helping us more. At that point no one would lend us a room to practice after school. Yolanda started talking about resigning. We didn't want her to go. She was the only one who would fight with anyone for our rights, but at the end they fired her. I think they fired her because we started to rebel against the principal's rules. The *cholos* [gang members] threatened to break classroom windows if they fired her.

Finally, Yolanda was asked to leave the school for her role beyond that of nurse's assistant. The artistic group disintegrated and, according to Carla, minority students began to lose interest in the school and its activities and many of them dropped out of school.

On another interview, I asked Carla if she remembered any mentor after her post-dropout experience at the rural school. Carla remembered the school's bilingual coordinator, Ms. Heckman, another important advocate during her senior year at Mountain High. Ms. Heckman had never been Carla's teacher, but Carla remembered that it was because of her prompt intervention that she was able to graduate from high school. Ms. Heckman not only resolved a grade conflict and complaint Carla had against her senior English teacher, but later she even recommended Carla's application for college. Carla felt she was very fortunate to have found Ms. Heckman. She described her as a person who "resolved problems instead of creating them." During her senior year, Carla faced yet another obstacle. This time it was a disagreement over a failing grade the teacher in her sheltered, senior ESL had given her. Ms. Rodriguez claimed she failed Carla for not having handed in several assignments. With a failing grade, Carla was unable to graduate with the rest of her classmates. Carla argued that she had turned in all of her assignments on time.

According to Carla, Ms. Rodriguez had a reputation for being disorganized and rather untidy with students' work. Anticipating a problem, Carla visited Ms. Rodriguez' classroom assistant, who, after checking her computer, confirmed that Carla's assignments had been all turned in and graded:

> It was Ms. Rodriguez's assistant who told me to fight for my rights. She said that Ms. Rodriguez had failed other students in the past for no reason at all. Her own assistant was tired of students complaining, and she promised to help me.

Carla, who had never before made a complaint against a teacher, went to see her teacher's immediate supervisor, Ms. Heckman. Remembering her past and the event that led her to drop out of school, Carla said, "This time, no one would stop me from graduating." Ms. Heckman "spoke Spanish and was very sympathetic to the needs of Mexican students," Carla explained. Apparently, this was not the first time Carla's teacher had received a complaint. Therefore, Carla's case was channeled to the office of the principal who ordered a grade investigation. In the end, Carla was given the grade she deserved and her teacher was reprimanded.

Carla was well aware that without the power of Ms. Heckman who believed in her and took her case to the principal her complaint would not have been resolved. In her opinion, minority students need advocates but the trick, she said, "is to find them." I asked Carla what she would have done if she had not found a mentor or if this situation had taken place when she first arrived in the United States with limited English skills. She replied:

> If I hadn't found the bilingual coordinator who helped me, I'd gone to the principal's office and had waited for him outside the door until he could talk to me. Now, I have learned that even if you can't speak English, there are other ways. I have changed. I wasn't as aggressive in the past.

Bilingual Education: "Thanks to That We Passed the Classes"

As Carla mentioned before, throughout her high school education (in both her rural and urban high schools) she was placed in sheltered classes and ESL segregated environments. Separated physically and psychologically from her majority Anglo peers, Carla was unable to challenge the stereotypes held by her majority peers. This separation was emotionally painful not only because it kept her in a state of social isolation but mainly because the curricula also conveyed the idea that her limited English skills were the equivalent of her being intellectually inferior.

The stratified academic environment supported Carla's conclusion that both the disciplinary system and the segregated curriculum contributed to keeping Mexican students on the failing track. Teachers also corroborated and provided Carla evidence that academic ability varied along ethnic lines. Carla's Anglo peers were placed in "honors" classes and given higher-level instruction, whereas Carla's remedial classes were for the most part not motivating or academically oriented. Carla remembered some of the teachers in her bilingual program at her urban high school. Some read newspapers or ate their lunch during class while Carla filled out handouts copying answers from a book:

> Our bilingual biology teacher, he would always bring milk and a sandwich to class to eat. He would sit at his desk and tell us to read from the book and fill out handouts or puzzles. That was every day. He had his assistant grade papers and he wouldn't even take attendance. Someone else would do it for him. We knew he was lazy. In our bilingual government class, the teacher who was an Anglo

would always bring his newspaper to read. We would be watching a movie or answering questions from a book. I didn't learn in those bilingual classes.

As I listened to Carla, I understood some of the reasons behind the decreasing popularity of bilingual education programs among mainstream and even some Latino families in recent years. Since I was an educator in the same urban high school in which Carla was completing her senior year, I knew well the "bilingual educators" she was referring to. I knew that Carla's statements were not exaggerated or magnified, and I knew that such "bilingual educators" were a discredit to the profession as well as to the bilingual education community. Their mediocre teaching reputation and desire to retire in a few years were well known within the school. However, the satisfactory professional evaluations they would receive every year from their supervisors were truly inexplicable.

When school administrations and school districts genuinely believe in the benefits of bilingual programs, their concern for their success is manifested in hiring effective teachers. Carla expressed the real expectation of her school regarding the success of bilingual programs:

> We were all Mexicans or Chicanos in those classes. Maybe that was the reason these teachers did not care to teach well. The school did not care to look into what this teacher was doing in class with us.

Latino students, in general, and Mexican immigrants, in particular, tend to identify their teachers as members of an "extended family." This respect for the role and authority of a teacher impeded their questioning the decisions teachers make during instruction. Knowing that their decisions were not going to be questioned by the students, and perceiving Latino students as academically inferior, teachers exercised pedagogical methods that appeared to create internal school stratification and academic marginalization. In Carla's bilingual classes vertical, teacher-dominated, whole group instruction was the norm in instruction. Individual opportunities for interactions with the teacher or group cooperative activities were not practiced. Learning was inhibited in bilingual classrooms, greatly limiting opportunities for critical thinking, creativity, and academic engagement.

The perceptions of some of Carla's bilingual teachers on Latino students, reinforced by the media and popular beliefs, were at times harmful to students' self-esteem. That was the case in the following incident that Carla shared with me in one of our last sessions and after we had established substantial rapport. During her senior year, Carla was placed in a class taught by a bilingual Latino teacher with an Anglo last name. As the class became more challenging, Carla's teacher recommended that she stay after school to receive tutorial sessions. Carla, who was determined to graduate, agreed to the tutorial program at least twice a week. Carla explained:

The teacher sat next to me on a table. As he was explaining something he placed his hand over my hand and began moving my pencil. Then, he put his hand on my leg. I remember the way he would look at me. I was wearing a skirt that day and we were alone in his room. He did it again, first it was my knee, then higher. I got so scared I jumped up, and told him I was leaving. We thought he was a nice and friendly teacher but yeah he would always look at girls in a special way, in certain parts. I said to myself "I don't care if I fail that class I will not go to tutoring classes no more." I was very scared. I told my friends the next day and two of my girlfriends said they had had the same problem with him.

Carla did not report this incident to the school authorities for fear they would not believe her. She confided that this teacher still works at the school and was even promoted. Carla felt that Mexican girls were stigmatized by some teachers and by their majority peers. They believed that "all Mexican girls would eventually get pregnant and drop out," she said. Carla began to have mixed feelings about the value of being part of a bilingual program. Most of her bilingual teachers imparted watered-down, unengaging instruction. For the most part, they were veteran teachers who did not transmit enthusiasm or a love for learning. The methods used were not the most efficient or backed by successful bilingual research. Carla's teachers used English textbooks, tested in English, and occasionally lectured in Spanish. This strategy, according to Carla, was not beneficial when it came to being assessed in the dominant language. Carla explained:

> All my classes were bilingual, history, biology, math, government. Our textbooks were English and we were tested in English as well but the teachers were all bilingual. They would speak Spanish sometimes, especially when they'd tell jokes. I'd have preferred to be placed in regular classes because in these bilingual classes I didn't learn anything.

With all the years of her academic exposure to different school environments, Carla was able to distinguish between a good bilingual class and a bad or mediocre one. During one of my interviews with her, she talked about a bilingual program that was very effective in the initial stages of her English language development:

> I remember a bilingual class I enjoyed. The teachers work together in a team. In the morning, the science lesson was explained in Spanish, and they'd give us some vocabulary to learn in English. In the afternoon, with a gringo teacher, we'd receive the same class in English. It was great because we'd understand everything. It made sense in English after we had heard it in Spanish.

Carla felt that if she had continued with such bilingual classes, she would have met the standards of Mexican schools. According to Carla, graduates from Mexico are academically more advanced in math and science than

their north-of-the-border counterparts. She claimed she was able to corroborate this academic disparity during her subsequent visits to relatives in Mexico. She said:

> What we learn here in grade 12, they are learning in Mexico in grade 9 or 10. There are things I was learning in math or science when I was a senior and my friends in Nogales had already studied in grade 10, and they helped me with homework. When I first came to the United States I was placed in seventh grade. What they taught me I had already learned it in Mexico in fifth grade. It was a bit hard for me because I didn't speak English.

In sum, Carla seemed to suggest that to be successful our schools cannot overlook the need to provide ongoing training for high school teachers. Much of the success of a school lies in the hands of those directly responsible for implementing school programs. She also seemed to indicate that schools need to re-evaluate their selective standards. Whether bilingual or not, school programs and teachers should hold the same high expectations for academic achievement for all students. Bilingual education programs in the twenty-first century should be perceived and implemented as enriched instruction open to gifted and talented students from all ethnic groups. As Crawford (2000) argued, we do not live in the World War I era, a period when learning other languages in schools came to be associated with disloyalty to the United States. In the midst of serious world globalization efforts in which many countries are united through a common currency and in which other nations enforce policies to officialize bilingualism, the United States should move to develop its language resources in a positive and not a substractive manner.

Success: "It Has Many Dimensions"

On a different interview, Carla and I talked about the meaning of the word *success*. The word success for Carla had many meanings: "You cannot claim to be successful if you have not satisfied all your aspirations at every level." She defined success as the process of achieving all your goals at the professional, spiritual, and personal levels. She did not limit success to accomplishing academic aspirations. For her, living in harmony with family and friends was as important as satisfying intellectual goals or becoming financially independent. At the time of the interview, Carla felt that she was successful at the personal level. She had the love and support of her family and friends, but she was striving to succeed at the academic level. Carla said she would be successful the day she becomes a school teacher: "Right now I'm satisfied at the personal level. My family is very united and they care for me. One day I will have a career, a job and be successful at that level as well."

The themes in Carla's worldview indicated an orientation toward the spiritual rather than exclusively toward the material and instrumental levels.

Her view of success was related to the fulfillment of her need to help others and to be able to earn a living doing something she enjoyed:

> To be successful for me is to be satisfied with what I am doing. To help the children in my case. I'd like to be a teacher and feel useful. To teach the kids the things they haven't taught me. . . . But mainly success for me is to be able to do what I enjoy doing.

Carla's successive negative incidents with teachers, poor instruction, and the school's low expectations have fortunately driven her to seek a teaching career in which she could offer children what she did not receive. But she also believed there were other ways to accomplish aspirations besides academia. In her world, there were examples of close relatives who had reached their objectives through hard work and self-motivation. However, for her, college was the fastest way to obtain her goals. She was motivated toward a college degree to prove to herself and to her parents that she was able to achieve what no one believed she could accomplish: "My parents always believed I was a party girl, and that I only liked to play. In part, I want to prove them wrong."

In one of our interviews, I asked Carla to give me a few examples of the obstacles she thought were constraining her success. Added to all the information mentioned before, Carla responded that her parents did not place a high priority on her education:

> I love my parents and they are very nice in many ways, but I wish they were like other parents I have seen that participate more actively in the education of their children. My parents did not push me to study. They wouldn't say, "Study." You will have these or these benefits. It was the same for them whether I studied or not. That's why I lost two years after I dropped out and stayed home. They wouldn't motivate me; they were rather indifferent.

Carla's mother dropped out of school because she needed to work to help her family. From both the paternal and maternal side, Carla had only one relative, an aunt, who graduated from college. I heard resentment in Carla's voice when she said that her aunt would have been her ideal mother.

Identity: "Mexicans and Chicanos Look Alike; Cholos Are Different"

The following theme provided a description of Carla's own construction of her *persona*. Carla's testimony manifested an ongoing struggle to try to succeed academically without "selling out." She seemed to claim that she needed the space and support necessary to express her emerging self and her immigrant identity.

First, Carla compared her orientation and behavior to that of Latinos born in the United States. Throughout her schooling experience, she interacted with both academically engaged and disengaged Mexicans and Latinos born in the United States. Their academic orientation, she said, depended on their individual past relationship with the school and their strength of character to overcome obstacles. She discarded the notion that involuntary Latino minorities were less successful than Mexican immigrants:

> I have seen many Mexicans immigrants like me who dropped out and were not interested in school anymore. They let the obstacles overwhelm them. There are many Chicanos who do good in school too. I say that it depends on the experience each student has had with the school, his teachers, his family, and the determination you have.

Carla felt that both Chicanos and Mexican-born Latinos have similar worldviews and cultural traits. However, she was emphatic when making a distinction between Chicanos and *cholos:*

> I have encountered two types of Chicanos: The ones who speak Spanish, have the same family values, enjoy the same music as us, dress like us, walk like us. They just think like us but they speak better English. The other group, the *cholos,* they are different. There is a big difference between a *cholo* and a Chicano. A *cholo* is a person with a lot of problems.

Carla believed that *cholos* have social adaptation problems. They were easily identified by the way they dressed and behaved. They were normally the students involved in gang-related activities and the ones who had no family support. In spite of ideological and cultural commonalities, Carla felt that Mexicans had a more difficult relationship with the system than Latinos born here because of their English language handicap:

> If I had come to the United States when I was a little girl, I'd have spoken better English, I'd have had less problems. People don't socialize with you when you don't speak good English. That happened to me when I first came.

The necessity of English comprehension for social participation and societal integration was the message always transmitted to Carla. Therefore, she believed that societal discrimination is much stronger when you have not mastered English:

> I think discrimination is stronger because of language. The gringos at school did not associate with us because we couldn't speak English well. Now, that my English is better, at least they respond to me.

I asked Carla if she believed that African Americans or Chicanos were discriminated even when language was not a factor for these groups. After reflecting she answered:

> Yes. People also discriminate you for your color and especially for your social class. In Mexico, there is racism and discrimination but I think here there is more. Chicanos are accepted to a certain extent because they speak English, but they are criticized and looked down at. And Blacks have a history with the gringos that comes from way back.

I asked Carla what differences she perceived between herself and an African American:

> I feel the same in the sense that they are discriminated against and so are we. However, they carry a deeper resentment against the gringos than we do. They are more hurt. There are many of us, Mexicans, that don't feel inferior to any gringo, but the Blacks still do. That's why they are so loud and outspoken. They want to call the attention of the gringos, tell them, "We are here." In that sense we are different.

I then asked Carla to define the differences or similarities she found between herself and a European-American student. Carla did not see major differences between Anglos or Latinos other than physical differences. She believed both groups are equipped with the same intelligence and talents. However, Carla related that academically Anglos tended to prefer to "work alone." In terms of ideology and racial relations, Carla had witnessed in high school that Anglo students were less likely to socialize with ethnic minorities than their African-American counterparts. She explained:

> I think a gringa and I are the same. Our only difference is our skin color and eyes. If a gringa likes to study, you will also find a Mexican girl who enjoys studying. You will also find crazy girls in every race. Maybe one difference is that they prefer to work alone. I think though that the gringos are more racist. It is hard to see a gringa in the halls walking with a Black girl. It is easier to see a Mexican girl walking with a Black girl.

Referencing literature that documents that school and classroom factors influence students' identities, I asked Carla if the school and curriculum provided her with any opportunity to express or assert her identity. My interest was in exploring if schools provided opportunities to integrate Latino culture forms of expression with traditional pro-academic mainstream activities. She responded that she did not remember any class in which they had the opportunity to discuss issues about their culture or about their interactions with peers from other races. She revealed that I was the only educator she knew that had demonstrated any interest in her heritage, place of birth, or past schooling experiences. She continued:

> My teachers only knew I was a Mexican and that's about it. No one had ever asked me about my family or my schools in Mexico, I don't think they cared. I just remember a time when a counselor came and we talked a bit about the frequent ethnic fights at school. She just told us to report the students who initiated the fights, but we did not have an opportunity to express our feelings.

Later, we talked about the holidays and celebrations honored by the school, and she remembered an incident that exacerbated the sensitivity of Latinos at the large urban high school. A group of students had requested the school administration to organize an assembly honoring the Mexican 5 de Mayo celebration. The school administration agreed under the condition that such assembly be opened only to Mexican students in bilingual programs. Carla explained:

> We were in the big auditorium and the Mariachi and folklorico dancers were going to perform. So everyone was excited and began to yell, "Viva Mexico." So a teacher and an administrator came to the microphone to tell us to stop yelling that phrase or else they were going to suspend the assembly. We protested against their rules. It made no sense for us. If we were celebrating a Mexican holiday, why couldn't we celebrate Mexico? There was nothing wrong with what we were saying. I didn't see the point in organizing the assembly. At the end, they always win. The assembly was stopped.

Demonstrations of ethnic allegiance were obviously not welcomed in school. Students read in these rules unwelcoming messages on the part of school authorities. Latino youth from then on, said Carla, felt compelled to hide their ethnic and racial selves and remain in their segregated environments.

Racial Conflicts: "On Each Corner Divided by Color"

The first thought that entered Carla's mind when I asked her what changes she would implement if she were a school administrator was related to racial conflicts. Emphatically, Carla pointed out that her first impression of an urban high school was that of groups of students divided by race in different corners of the patio during school lunch:

> When I first came to Mountain High, I was puzzled to see races clearly divided standing in the patio at lunch time. Anglos with Anglos, Mexicans with Mexicans, Blacks with Blacks. I remembered asking my first friends at school the rea-

son for the division. They'd tell me that it was the way groups defended from each other. "This school has a long tradition for racial fights," they would say.

Carla narrated several violent racial confrontations she had witnessed during her senior year at Mountain High:

> I saw many fights at lunch time. One time it was between Anglos, the "skin heads," and Mexicans. But it is always the same thing. The ones who were punished and suspended were the Mexicans. Other times there were fights between Chicanos and Mexicans and Blacks and Mexicans.

What puzzled Carla the most was the fact that, in spite of the years of racial unrest, the school administration had not created programs or classes to promote cultural understanding and learning. School authorities concentrated their energies in suspending or expelling the individuals involved, most of the time in an "unfair and biased way," Carla claimed. Opportunities for students to learn about each other were nonexistent and most students were segregated into their own cultural worlds:

> I was surprised that the school did not do something, maybe organizing activities so we could all create friendships. I know that the school was so big that it was probably difficult to handle, but at least they should have done something to stop the isolation. I would have liked to have friends from other races. It was the first time I had seen something like that. Nobody would do anything.

Carla praised the unity and loyalty among African-American staff members and students. She perceived qualities that were not often found among Latinos when confronted with conflicts against other races. She recalled having witnessed one of the worst racial conflicts among students, staff members, and even a few teachers the year she was graduated. This particular school fight got the attention of the media when over 20 police cars came to the scene to help. Carla recalled:

> When there are fights the Black monitors defend the Black students and report the adversaries; they defend their race. One day, we were all having lunch. The fight was in the news on TV, remember? About 20 police cars came. I was there, and I saw how the Chicano monitors were kicking the Mexicans. But the Black teachers were defending the Black students. There are only a few Mexican teachers that I know that promote unity among the Latino students. All the others go against their race. When the fight ended, there were about 12 arrests, most of them were Mexicans, one Black. They didn't arrest the gringos and there were many of them involved.

Carla's testimony was clear and objective. For her, ethnic loyalty and justice are important qualities that she did not witness at school. She was well aware of the areas in which Latinos needed more reflection and growth. She knew that Mexicans are divided and often do not support their own race as other groups do. She concluded, "We needed someone neutral at school."

Good Teachers: "I Must First Find Out Each Teacher's Reputation"

During our final interview Carla had already enrolled in a community college. It was her first semester and she intended to become a bilingual educator. I wanted her to talk about her college life and the differences she encountered there in comparison with her urban high school. She commented that the problems experienced in high school had taught her many lessons: "Now, I ask about the reputation of an instructor before enrolling in a class." She seemed thrilled with the fact that in college the students have the option to select their courses each semester:

> I can pick the classes I prefer and select the hours I can come to college. I think that it's great. Especially because I live an hour away from the community college. I remember in high school, we had to take the classes they would give us. Generally art, home economics, those kinds of classes. If I wanted to take computers, the counselors would say there was no space. Here, I am taking a computer class now.

Carla is profoundly convinced that college is a "different world." When I asked her what classes taken in high school were useful for her in a college, she responded:

> The truth is that I can't answer you that question. I don't think I learned anything in high school that is helping me now. Can't you believe me when I tell you that my teacher here is tutoring me after class time? I don't even know the proper way to write an essay. We never learned how to write an essay in high school. In ESL classes we just copied answers from a book. Here they are making us think.

Students' voices, like the one of Carla's, reveal to us the ways schools organize and select knowledge. Patterns that emanate from selective tracking seem to indicate that Latinos are usually destined to occupy the nonacademic tracks.

Conclusion

Although Carla felt powerless as a newly emigrated Mexican to change or control the American schooling system that was stripping her of her cultural identity, she did manage to graduate from high school and go to a community college. Carla had the advantage of a strong identity rooted in her family life and upbringing in Mexico. She recognized the symbolic power of language and how it was being manipulated and managed by the dominant forces to control and resocialize her and her Mexican immigrant counterparts attending schools in the United States.

Carla remained staunchly opposed to pressures to assimilate rapidly. This is nowhere more evident than in her refusal to speak only English. In fact, she expended considerable effort to use her language whenever she could, especially in school, even though she learned to speak and write English well enough to later succeed in community college studies.

Carla's worst moments in high school came when she encountered teachers who abused their authority, stereotyped students, or were overtly hostile toward recent immigrants like herself. The exercise of strict disciplinary rules that differed from those of the school environment she was accustomed to in Mexican schools resulted in her dropping out of school for two years. She was not only strongly affected but also deeply hurt by the teachers of her own race who were most uncaring and unsupportive of the needs of limited English students. Such teachers created a school environment in which she felt constrained in expressing her ethnic self and which made her feel unwelcome and not respected. She felt that although American schools preach ethnic democracy and equal opportunity, they, in fact, actually create strong distinctions based on race that add to racial tensions in the schools. Her account of placement in ESL classes, separated from the mainstream student body, highlighted this as a personal experience. She highlighted the importance of putting an end to the social and racial isolation rampant in urban school environments that perpetuates conflicts and misunderstanding between groups.

Carla struggled to maintain her identity and at the same time succeed academically. After returning to high school the second time, she again encountered many obstacles that almost impeded her high school graduation. However, she was an outgoing young woman who learned from the system how to survive and succeed. She found advocates who not only provided emotional support but also were willing to use their power as professional staff to assist her. Fortunately, she was able to identify such key people at critical times during her high school career.

Obvious incidents of academic tracking, mediocre programs, nonsupportive teachers, and other covert yet direct messages sent by the school through its policies and procedures almost defeated Carla in her quest for educational opportunities. It is little wonder that an immigrant would experience considerable discontinuity. Ultimately, her testimony, especially her accounts about schooling in Mexico compared to schooling in the United States, revealed the stark differences in the socialization processes and cultural environments inherent in the two systems. For Carla, the Mexican system reflected the personal involvement of an extended family, whereas the American system stressed individualism and competition. Carla, as an immigrant, had a basis for comparison and could devise survival strategies that ultimately served her well. It seems that her early school experiences in Mexico may, in fact, have helped her to retain the pride and dignity she needed while the American system was trying to force her rapid assimilation.

FOR DISCUSSION

1. Provide some specific examples in which Carla manifested her "oppositional identity" and affirmed her loyalty to her language and culture. Does Carla's case demonstrate that issues of race and identity should be handled appropriately in school? Should they become part of the school curriculum or are they too complex to discuss with students? Take a stand and defend your position.

2. Carla's statement "I want to teach the children the things they haven't taught me" reveals her disappointment with an educational system that did not meet her expectations. After reading this chapter, what programs and practices implemented in the schools Carla attended do you think she is referring to? In Carla's opinion, what are the characteristics of a good school and a good curriculum?

3. What kind of teachers most impressed Carla? What differences does she find between Mexican teachers and educators born in the United States?

4. Provide some examples of positive or collaborative interactions Carla found with her teachers. Then provide some specific examples of negative or coercive interactions she encountered with teachers or school administrators. Which were more frequent in Carla's school experience?

5. If you were a school administrator, what kind of programs, policies, and practices would you implement to allow students the opportunity to affirm their identity and to succeed in school? How would you diminish the impact of negative interactions between students and some of their teachers?

6. In Carla's opinion, how did the schools she attended in the United States promote cultural understanding and learning among the diverse racial groups? What are Carla's views on the African-American community in contrast with the Mexican and Latino groups? In what ways do interracial conflicts in schools affect students' views about themselves and their desire to succeed academically?

7. What programs or practices would you incorporate in the school curriculum to create mutual understanding and learning across diverse groups? What existing programs have such goals?

8. Living in a rural community where public transportation was not available, Carla had to rely on a school bus that picked her up before 6:00 a.m. (one and a half hours before the start of the school day). This created a problem for Carla who also had to assist her younger siblings get ready for school. The continuous

threats of the principal due to her lack of punctuality caused her to drop out of school. Play the role of the district's superintendent, the school principal, Carla's parents, and her teacher and act out or write a scenario in which the problem is satisfactorily resolved.

9. Manny's and Carla's classrooms encouraged independent learning and competition instead of collaborative projects that were in tune with the students' culturally based learning styles. Imagine you were hired to teach a group of 30 students whose learning styles are similar to those of Carla and Manny. With a friend, elaborate 5 different lesson plans that incorporate collaborative methodologies and projects. Indicate the academic tasks of each of the students in the groups and the way you will assess them.

10. How does Carla interpret academic success? Why did she return and graduate?

11. Given Carla's testimony and the negative interactions with some of her teachers, we can assume that teacher training programs are needed. What would be the characteristics of a program you would implement for teachers if you were a school administrator?

5 Introducing the Educators

In this chapter, educators' responses to a questionnaire shed light on a number of issues on the purposes of educating Latino youth. In particular, responses to this questionnaire revealed beliefs about who should teach Latino studies and about the constraints Latino youths face in achieving educational equality. Success for Latinos was expressed as being derived from many sources and given many definitions. This chapter provides a basis for comparing the views of educators with the views of students.

As part of this study, high school educators and administrators working in Carla's and Manny's schools responded to a questionnaire. It contained 12 open-ended questions designed to elicit views relevant to Latino students and their education. Of the 33 educators responding to the questionnaire, 10 were Latinos, 20 were Anglos, and 3 were African Americans. These educators were representative of the faculty's ethnic makeup of the school under study. The findings in this chapter are based on a thematic analysis of these responses. Words and phrases used in common by the respondents were tabulated and organized under themes representing the 12 questions asked. The themes generally represent the most widely held views, or the "middle ground," although there was considerable variation in the written answers. Opinions of some of the more outspoken "outliers" are presented in a discussion of the themes, especially when clearly divided views were expressed.

"They Don't Seem to Fit"

Question 1: What are the major issues facing Latino students today? The primary issues identified were language, poverty, and discrimination. Most mainstream educators who responded to the questionnaire highlighted *language* as the main issue facing Latino students. Thus, language was their primary measure of students' potential. Teachers' perceptions of students' poor language often produce negative expectations about students' personalities and academic capabilities. If we are discussing bicultural students or those for whom English is a second language, teachers often overlook substantial research (Cummins, 2000), which indicates that it takes 5 to 7 years for students to acquire an adequate academic language to handle school classroom activities. In addition, teachers who used the students' native language in high school reading and writing activities as a bridge to develop English academic skills were almost nonexistent in Carla's and Manny's schools. An Anglo female English teacher with 10 years of experience addressed language issues:

> The biggest problem facing Latino students is the fact that most of them cannot read and write in English or Spanish by the time they get out of high school.

Another mainstream teacher responded in a more holistic way about the challenges that Latino students face in schools. He linked language issues directly to the frustration of school failure and then to the larger social issues that created this frustration in the first place:

> Students of Latino, Mexican-American, or Chicano heritage are faced with many challenges. One of these issues is learning academic or standard English. It is not surprising that a student who is born in the United States does not express in correct written or verbal form. This is a contribution of school frustration that could lead to failure. Other issues pertinent to academics could be discrimination, equal job and education opportunities, and social–economic poverty.

A Mexican-American language arts teacher expanded on the link between schools and the larger society. She noted that social issues weigh heavily on Latino students at the same time they are facing the developmental issues experienced by all youth:

> Schools are a microcosm of the surrounding communities. The stresses and problems in the surrounding population will be reflected in the students, whether they be economic, social–political, or any of the social ills that beleaguer society as a whole. In addition, students of all ages face the normal challenges in human social and psychological development as they transition from childhood into adulthood. In attempting to identify the major issues in Latino school education one cannot ignore the impact of the larger social problems they and their families face in the outside world.

There were some Mexican-American educators who responded that cultural domination was a "major issue." One Mexican-American teacher opened the narrative of his questionnaire with the summation that the most far-reaching issue facing Latino students is "the eradication of their language, their culture and the suppression of their minds." In a similar vein, another Mexican-American male teacher with 10 years of experience who taught American government and history stated that the greatest issue is that "Latinos are in culture shock":

> Latino students find themselves surrounded by issues that are difficult to understand. To begin with, Latinos are in culture shock because they're in strange

surroundings due to their migration to the land of their great-grandfathers which is now inhabited by strange people who don't understand their cultures.

An experienced Mexican-American male administrator, while agreeing that language issues predominate, also hinted that some of the negative social issues affecting Latinos are reflective of a nonresponsive curriculum. This Latino high school administrator in Arizona who advocated for bilingual and multicultural educational programs expressed his concern in this way:

> One major issue facing Latino students is having equal access to the curriculum because of a lack of English proficiency. In those cases, bilingual education is needed. Many times Latino students are English speakers but the curriculum or the text and materials used do not reflect them. They cannot see themselves in the curriculum or in the instruction and hence they are alienated and given to the understanding that they are not necessarily wanted in our schools.

His answer is consistent with Manny's testimonies in Chapter 3. As Manny stated, his history class was taught "from the White man's perspective" and did not acknowledge the contributions of other groups to the building of the nation. The only class he enjoyed, Literatures of the Southwest, was offered one semester and was then quickly removed from the school curriculum.

In analyzing the first question regarding the major issues affecting Latinos today, three general groupings of responses were identified. The first group of answers includes responses that identify some form of negative pathology presumed to be afflicting the students or their communities, such as "drugs" and "laziness." These were coded as "P." The second grouping were "psycho-social" responses, such as "lack of knowledge of native language" and "do not connect school with future." These were coded "PS." The third grouping included social-institutional issues. These included such comments as "discrimination" and "teachers' lack of cultural understanding of students." These were coded "SI." Table 5.1 indicates that Anglo teachers

TABLE 5.1 Number and Frequency of Responses to Question 1

	Classifications of Teacher Responses					
	Social Institutional		Pathological		Psycho-social	
Ethnicity	Freq.	%	Freq.	%	Freq.	%
Anglo	5	16%	20	63%	7	22%
Latino	12	39%	10	32%	9	29%
African American	3	50%	1	17%	2	33%

Note. Total: $N = 33$; Anglos: $n = 20$; Latinos: $n = 10$; African Americans: $n = 3$

tended to identify students and community "pathologies" as major issues, whereas, Hispanics identified "social-institutional" issues. African Americans tended to identify psycho-social issues.

"These Kids Need Role Models"

Question 2: What qualities/kinds of persons are needed to address these issues? The answers largely indicated that Latino students need good teaching from culturally sensitive teachers. However, the single need most often mentioned by the respondents was more Hispanic leaders and role models both within the school and the community. There were several different perspectives on the argument for role models. An Anglo teacher indicated that positive role models were needed to counteract negative influences on Hispanic youth:

> These kids need role models in the schools, the community, and media. They need to be engaged in worthwhile causes that improve their lot. They need to have other than social causes to celebrate.

Another Anglo teacher linked the need for role models to larger social issues and the need for better modeling of positive learning behaviors in the school and community. She did not want to highlight any special needs Latino students have. In her view, all children have similar needs. She saw the issues affecting Hispanics as also a general need in society:

> I think all society needs to address these issues. Young people, regardless of their race, need parental guidance, teachers who model integrity, and a more responsible media that does not push sex and momentary pleasure as the ultimate goals in life. We need people of integrity and morals and we hold that up for our young people. They need to see their role models advocate a love of reading, writing, speaking, and listening for all children.

One Latino teacher argued for "fair shares" and equality in reflecting diversity in the teaching ranks in proportion to the student population. This again suggests a need for more role models:

> We need teachers who are representative of the same background as the students. The teaching force needs to reflect the student population and we also need teachers who are sensitive and understand the needs of the students. The "boot strap" philosophy is not necessarily going to help our students stay in school; they need encouragement and support to be able to succeed.

The voice of this Latino educator belies the alarming shortage of minority teachers in urban schools in the United States. According to the National Education Association (NEA), urban schools in the United States are facing a

73% shortage of bilingual teachers. In addition, 42% of urban schools in the nation do not have an Hispanic educator (National Education Association, 2000). According to another private publication (Recruiting New Teachers [RNT], 2000) two million new teachers are needed in the next few years. The severe shortage of educators falls in critical subject areas, especially at the high school level. For example, the teacher shortage in the field of English as a Second Language is at 68%, and the shortage in math is at 95%.

In addition to the need for more Spanish-speaking educators in schools, Mexican-American educators suggested that some of the larger social dynamics that create social and political repression for Hispanics need to be addressed. They tended to view Latino students as needing people in their lives who are aware of these issues and can help students deal with them. One male teacher explained that Latino students need "a person whose goals are to create life within our Chicano youth; and create a learning environment that promotes and provokes thought." Another said, "Perhaps people of the same culture and language. People must not only understand the issues but understand them emphatically."

The responses to this question were grouped into three areas. The first group of responses clearly identified teachers as a powerful influence and that they need certain qualities if Latino students are to succeed. The second group identified a combination of teacher attributes and attributes of external people and forces. The final group identified external people—such as role models in the community—as pivotal. Clearly, most of the educators view themselves as one of the most powerful forces that affect the lives of Latino youth. Since the responses were fairly uniform across all ethnic groups, the groups represented do not distinguish the ethnicity of the respondents.

"Si Se Puede"

Question 3: What do Latino students need to learn in order to address these issues? The most frequent response was not only the need to commit to education and to learn the attitudes needed to succeed in education, but also the need to understand where Latino students fit in the overall fabric of American society. An Anglo teacher said:

> Latino students need to have the basic skills and higher-order learning skills to be able to succeed in school. They need the discipline to acquire these skills.

The second most frequent response was generally represented in the views of the Hispanic respondents. This response related to the need to identify with and seek pride in Hispanic culture. In turn, culture serves as the substratum for positive self-esteem and the desire to succeed. An Hispanic administrator named the family as the source of identity and success:

Si Se Puede! Students need to know that anything the mind can conceive and believe, it can achieve. Pride in the familia determines to a large extent how one feels about him/herself. Confidence can be built by one's peers and family, but success in the early years of school is critical to the positive attitude needed to face tougher challenges. Your self-esteem and goal orientation will dictate how you bounce back from the numerous disappointments you will experience socially and academically in the formative years.

Another teacher believed that pride in one's culture was the link to success and the ability to deal with the dominant culture:

They need to learn to have pride in their own culture and at the same time not feel threatened by the dominant culture so that they can function successfully without losing their identity.

For the most part, educator's responses to this question fell into the psycho-social category. These included responses that indicated a psychological response or a social condition. For example "opportunities to grow" was an example of such a response.

A number of teachers indicated that students need specific skills, such as assertiveness to achieve academically in schools. The second group of responses included social power issues such as "function without losing identity." A higher percentage of Latinos than Anglos identified social powers and psycho-social issues as important, whereas a higher percentage of Anglos identified skills, education, and parent–community issues as important.

"A Belief That They Can Succeed"

Question 4: What do students need for self-fulfillment and development? This question elicited responses covering a wide range of social, personal, and academic skills factors. Two representative responses are as follows:

Students need social and affective motor skills that can enable them to face the realities and hardships of the real world. Examples of such skills could be conflict-resolving skills, self-esteem and self-confidence skills, and critical thinking skills, to name a few.

Critical thinking skills, vocabulary development, academic skills like study skills need to be taught, note-taking, "how to take a test" practice.

The second most frequent response related to better connections with the "real world." Responsible adults and students need to understand and develop themselves through better connections and interactions with their communities. An Anglo female teacher responded to the question in this way:

Students need to get out of "self" and develop a sense of community. "No man is an island." . . . They need to see that their own self-fulfillment comes from reaching out to others rather than selfishly grasping for MY RIGHTS. We need to stop focusing on "self-esteem" and focus on learning, working, helping others, etc. Self-esteem will be the natural outcome of these actions.

A third category of responses centered on the educational environment and its impact on the affective development of students. Three teachers indicated a variety of characteristics needed for such development:

A belief that they can succeed in this environment and that success does not mean being a traitor to their heritage.

Validation of themselves as human beings and of their culture. An understanding of their potential and encouragement to develop their potential.

They need to learn who they are, what they are, and what they can become. Students need to forget about Latino stereotyping of them and do whatever it takes to get an education. If it means working at a greasy spoon in order to fund their studies, that's what they have to do.

There were no clear groupings along ethnic lines in the responses to Question 4. Most of the responses related to preparing students for functioning in the "real world" and to developing a sense of self-worth. Most responses were consistent in the need for Latino students to become self-empowered and succeed. Interestingly, the questionnaire asked educators to provide specific examples of the ways they felt students could achieve their needs for self-fulfillment and development. For the most part, their answers did not indicate how the school, the curriculum, or teachers themselves could support students in achieving these goals.

"No, But Then Few, If Any, Public Schools Are"

Question 5: Is this school providing this type of learning? The majority of the teachers indicated that schools were not, or were only partially, meeting these needs. Many responses indicated that the system tended to preserve the status quo. Other educators revealed frustration because of the multiple nonacademic tasks that educators must perform today. These tasks, they said, do not leave them much time to offer an academically challenging curriculum for the growing numbers of nonmainstream students:

The school curriculum has changed very little from the high schools of 30 years ago. Many would argue that schools have been charged with many more additional responsibilities for the students than in the past. As a result, the emphasis for a classroom teacher is removed from the "academic arena" and is more focused on the physical and emotional needs of these students. We are meeting their "very basic" needs, but not at the level that would produce the most benefit for the greatest number of students.

One teacher indicated that there is a wide separation between school administration and policies and genuine concern for the actual needs of students. His words strongly voiced his concerns about schools that do not listen to teachers' and students' points of view. According to several teachers across the ethnic groups represented, schools implement reforms in a monolateral way:

> No, but then few, in any public schools are. By and large, the policy-makers do not seem truly interested in much of anything besides maintenance of the status quo and/or responding to pressure groups. A major problem is that administrators do not routinely interact with pupils or the people who deliver educational services to them—the teachers. I believe any learning environment suffers when the opinions of the only elements required for learning to take place—teacher and student—are rarely taken into consideration, let alone have equitable weight to the arid input of those outside the learning process.

This educator's views are consistent with the voices of the two students in this study. Many of the school policies and bureaucratic regulations in urban schools serving large numbers of Latino students are implemented and enforced without the support and feedback of teachers, students, and families. In Chapter 3 we heard Manny talk about a senseless school tardy policy in which students were required to remain standing and facing a wall for an hour. As Manny stated, there are more imaginative and fruitful ways for schools to redirect students' behavior without the need to shame a youngster. School policies that are inadequately researched result in students disliking school and learning. At the same time, school policies exacerbate the problems they originally intended to solve.

Most educators, regardless of their ethnic background, felt that schools were not truly meeting the challenge of effectively helping Latino students academically. The majority of their responses reflected their loss of enthusiasm as they experienced difficult conditions in the school systems. Teachers' variations in commitment and enthusiasm may explain in part their attitudes about working collaboratively with Latino students and their families. Most felt powerless because school administrators, school boards, and state legislatures deny them a sense of control over their function as teachers. In bygone days, as these teachers stated, they had greater control over classroom processes and a curriculum that was more loosely defined than it is now. Current teaching accountability legislation and strict statutory teacher licensing restrict options utilized by teachers in today's classrooms. Thus, it is not surprising that 22% of the new teachers hired in urban schools in the nation abandon the profession during the first three years (National Center for Education Statistics, 2000).

"I Have Mixed Feelings"

Question 6: Do you think it is important to teach Latino and Mexican-American Studies? This question produced a greater diversity of responses than the other questions, although there were three general groupings of responses: a few who opposed the idea outright; those who wholeheartedly supported it; and those who provisionally or tentatively supported it and suggested a "melting-pot approach" to teaching ethnic studies. Although one respondent said no, he did leave the door open for having such courses available to all students:

> No, I do not think it is important to teach Latinos Mexican/American studies. I believe it could be an elective offered to all students.

Not unexpectedly, the supporters were mostly Latinos. Some of their comments indicated such classes and programs were needed to support a healthy identity and to empower Latino youth:

> As a Chicano, I am highly biased and not very objective in terms of this question. It is so important to learn who you are and where your people came from while you're still developing a sense of self. I am only now receiving this type of education and it is significant to my entire self as well as my ability to teach.

Another simply stated:

> Chicano studies courses are a necessary element in the empowerment of our Chicano youth.

Most of the Anglo and a few of the Latino respondents qualified their support by indicating that Latino studies should be either offered as an elective for all students or infused across the curriculum. Generally, Anglo teachers supported the "melting-pot" or the "color-blind" approach, asserting that Latino students' needs are much the same as other students' needs and that a multicultural course, not necessarily a Latino studies course, could be added to the curriculum. A few in this category believed that the overall curriculum has a great impact on development of identity and the promotion of student success and that the focus should be there:

> I think it is important to teach cultural diversity and appreciation to *all* students. It needs to be integrated throughout the curriculum.

A Latino male administrator, corroborating what Carla had stated in Chapter 4, argued that Latino students were segregated in schools. Another mentioned that Latinos crowded ESL classes, vocational classes, and remedial programs. He suggested more collaborative projects among students from all ethnic races instead of isolating them in ethnic studies courses. He noted:

> I have mixed feelings. As long as the Latino studies are infused throughout the curriculum and not in an isolated course, the opportunity for dialogue amongst all students is much greater. Latinos need to see themselves in the curriculum. I believe a better tool for appreciating the differences between Latinos and other students is to get them to work collaboratively on projects, enroll in classes with Anglo students. Working as part of a team toward a common goal and learning to respect and work with one another will reap long-term benefits.

"This Question Is Immense"

Question 7: What kinds of things should be taught? Most respondents did not provide a direct answer but acknowledged that something was missing for Latinos. Some teachers indicated a form of basic skills. One Anglo teacher felt that students leave school without practical work skills:

> I think there should be a right-to-work program for those students who will not be going on to a higher education.

Another male Anglo teacher also supported this notion, indicating that the curriculum should provide some foundation for occupations and careers that he felt might be suitable for some Latino students. Such courses, he indicated, were much needed but nonexistent in the curriculum of this large urban high school:

> Curriculums should be based and evaluated on the student's capacity and education levels to determine what to teach them. We can't all be doctors and engineers and lawyers, but there is a call for other professions which are also rewarding where a child might excel and make good, but it all has to be based on his intelligence levels and his elementary education. You can't build a home without a foundation first.

Manny, the Latino student in Chapter 3, revealed his frustration with a school system that interprets success from a single reductionist perspective: the college option. The statements of the educator quoted above seem to agree with Manny's views. Schools need to provide a curriculum that recognizes and builds upon the skills and abilities that students bring with them, a curriculum that respects students' self-definition of success. Schools that use sorting mechanisms to devalue other valid forms of knowledge promote feelings of inadequacy and failure among bicultural youth.

An Anglo teacher reiterated the strong "melting-pot" or "assimilation" theme in the question about the *importance* of teaching Latino studies—that all students should somehow benefit, not just Latinos. His answer seemed to indicate that the rapid emergence of a multicultural society threatens the survival of homogenous American cultural and social views:

> A certain amount of homogeneity is necessary in society. Shared value systems enable us to have a confident faith in one another beyond ethnic boundaries. I understand that now there is no unitary national culture. Immigration has brought many people to the United States borders and certain freedoms sanctioned by this country have given a variety and flexibility to ethnic patterns. I believe it is necessary to adhere to a philosophy of education that does not cause that type of divisive segregation that results in "them versus us."

A female Anglo teacher recognized the importance of supporting the development of pride and dignity among students. However, she related this need primarily as a way to battle what she viewed as a negative pathology in the Latino community:

> This question is immense. I feel I will miss a significant area if I answer. I do know that pride and dignity are areas missing from the development of most students. Many students don't realize the historical significance of the Aztecs, the Mayas, or even Cesar Chavez. It is badly needed to develop an identity outside of the pachuco-gang [a southwestern term referring to a Mexican American with gang affiliations] identity that many students admire.

A Mexican-American male teacher was very incisive. He stated in a new way the theme contained in many of his survey responses that teaching students how to think is at the heart of issues in education for Latinos:

> The concepts of (a) self-empowerment, (b) the creation of thought being the nexus of the creation of life, (c) the essence of being a Chicano, and (d) the concept of Aztlan.

The majority of the Hispanic and the African-American respondents, along with many of the Anglo educators, saw Latino studies as a way in which to reinforce cultural identity and thought that they would have a positive effect on student success. As already noted, many of the Anglo respondents viewed the curriculum as needing to be oriented toward basic skills, such as reading, writing, and English language, because they felt that Latinos need more skill building than cultural reinforcement.

"It Does Not Make Any Difference What Ethnic Group the Teacher Belongs To"

Question 8: Who should teach Latino and Mexican-American studies? Anglos? Latinos? Why? This question evoked strong and opposing feelings. Issues of control and power surfaced among some educators. One Anglo male respondent strongly opposed to ethnic mentoring wrote:

> Who are you kidding? The idea that one race would teach something better than another sounds like it came from someone wearing a sheet.

Interestingly, only a couple of educators out of the 33 interviewed indicated that it would be best if Latinos taught such courses. The great majority indicated that members of other ethnic groups could also teach these courses if they were sufficiently qualified and interested:

> This class should be taught by the most qualified member of the staff, provided that the staff member is excited about teaching the class. It does not make a difference what ethnic group the teacher belongs to as long as the previous conditions are met.

The Latino respondents usually argued in some form for "fair shares" in being equally represented both in the curriculum and in the teaching force. Although they were open to the idea that non-Latinos could teach Latino studies, they also argued for overall equal ethnic representation in order to create and preserve a balance. An experienced Mexican-American male administrator who previously had publicly espoused Latino studies across the curriculum also said that Latinos should be proportionally represented in relation to the student body. In the school in which this survey was conducted there were visible inequalities between the majority Latino student population and the large mainstream faculty. He expressed his concern in this way:

> Latino and Mexican-American studies should be taught by all English and social studies teachers. The teaching force should reflect the student population. In other words, if we have 85% Latino or Mexican-American students in a school, 85% of the teaching force of that school or other faculty should also be of the same ethnic group. Latino or Mexican-American studies should not be exclusively provided to Latino or Mexican-American students because, again, it would give the impression that it is not legitimate and not the view held by everyone. So, all social studies and English teachers should be prepared to include this in their instruction.

In a similar vein, a Mexican-American teacher expressed the need for all students to learn about one another but also argued for a fair representation in the teaching force:

Education is all about understanding ourselves and others. I am a human being first, then a woman, then a Mexican American. I do not think I need to have lived in Ancient Egypt in order to share knowledge about that culture. While there may be some dimensions that would enhance my perception of my students because we are both Latinos that an Anglo cannot share, I do not believe a teacher of Latino studies would necessarily need to be Latino. However, I would worry if there were not Latino educators teaching these subjects at all.

A Latino male teacher recognized the talent and insight of teachers of other racial and ethnic backgrounds, but he also emphasized the need for easily recognizable role models for students:

I know that many people believe that only "Raza" [Spanish for race] can teach these classes, but I've met many wonderful teachers who eat, live, and breathe empowering Latino students. I can't imagine their talents can be totally ignored. On the other hand, seeing your own community in positions of authority and success can be so important. The right people need to teach these courses: sensitive, bright, and knowledgeable people.

Finally, another male Latino teacher emphasized individual "essence" and ability to teach how to think:

In my belief that anyone can be a Chicano, I believe anyone can teach Chicano studies. My main concern in a search for a teacher of Chicano studies would be the essence of the given teacher. Second, I would want a person who was going to promote the creation of thought.

The "melting-pot" theme remained consistent in the responses of most of the Anglo teachers. Most suggested that teachers, regardless of ethnicity, should have a hand in teaching about multiculturalism and that teaching should serve as a bridge between racial groups:

Everyone should teach multicultural studies after some instruction for the teachers. I believe having speakers available who are experts in certain areas is the ideal way to go. Also, a day scheduled so that speakers don't have to spend all day to speak to all of a teacher's classes.

And another summarized:

I think there should be a joint effort between Anglo and Hispanic teachers (team teaching) to provide a broader perspective and a bridge between racial and ethnic groups.

Table 5.2 provides the percentages of responses across ethnic groups.

TABLE 5.2   Number and Frequency of Responses to Question 8

| | Classifications of Teacher Responses | | | | | | | |
| | Latinos | | Any | | Joint | | Total | |
Ethnicity	Freq.	%	Freq.	%	Freq.	%	Freq.	%
Anglo	0	0%	18	100%	0	0%	18	100%
Latino	10	83%	2	17%	0	0%	12	100%
African American	1	33.3%	1	33.3%	1	33.4%	3	100%

Note. Total: $N = 33$; Anglos: $n = 20$; Latinos: $n = 10$; African Americans: $n = 3$

"Jumping Through a System of Hoops"

Question 9: What does "education" mean to you? What should it be? Should it be different from what it is? Answers to this question indicated that these educators' views of reality are far from the ideal. Many teachers indicated a need for radical changes to make education functional for students. One teacher said that the present system is severely outdated, which corroborated Manny's views in Chapter 3. Manny talked about "school as a waste of students' time." He explained how his school's outdated theoretical curriculum was not in tune with the reality of students' lives and killed their motivation to persevere academically. Manny spoke about the lack of community-based projects or "real-world" learning that he obtained through only a few vocational courses at school. In the same vein, the statements of this educator seem to reveal the urgent need for curriculum reform:

> The process of education (as a public school function) should certainly be different than it is. For purposes of simplification, suffice it to say that the segregated and compartmentalized approach prevalent in schools today (now we do reading, now we do math) needs to be changed. The majority of educational programs rely on a system of academic areas identified from the time of Greek universities. Certainly our populations, our students, and our needs today are quite distinct.

A Mexican-American teacher viewed education as largely preserving the status quo and social stratification. As I collected his questionnaire, I asked him if he had heard of Peter McLaren, Paolo Freire, Carlos Ovando, or Macedo, to which he answered no. Nevertheless, his response is at the heart of critical theory and pedagogy:

> Education is a means of self-evaluation and within education is the acquisition of knowledge, and through the acquisition of knowledge is the creation of a

higher and deeper degree of life. In terms of education within the educational system, it is a system that is used to create individuals who are without thought, who are lifeless, and who are prepared to take a position only at the bottom of the social, political, and educational ladder.

An Anglo teacher expressed this cynical reality:

> Jumping through a system of hoops to get a piece of paper. Doing things to get a grade not because you care. Not necessarily learning in the process. Memorization, cramming, boredom. Individualizing education to meet students' needs and interests could help make it better.

The educators' statements were in line with Carla's and Manny's perceptions of their education. Both students maintained that the emphasis on grades to comply with the school's grading policies prevented their teachers from ensuring that real learning was taking place. Manny spoke about the mechanization of learning and the teacher's overdependence on textbooks.

Some educators who participated in this study revealed their frustration with Arizona's move toward more state standardization and continuous testing. In their view, frequent testing is at odds with a stimulating learning experience. For many educators, learning and reading for pleasure are relegated to an exciting teaching practice of the past.

The teachers in this study who were less critical of the system said that education needed to have a "real-world" context. One teacher expressed the platonic concept of education while another focused on personal development and identity:

> To me, education means "drawing-out." We should be instilling important facts, but most importantly the ability to find information, interpret it, and work based on that information. I need to know about as many ideas as I can possibly learn about. I need to evaluate my ideas and adjust my life accordingly.

And another said:

> I think education should be developing the whole person, their skills, their understanding of the world around them, their value system, and their identity.

An Anglo respondent expressed the notion that the school's role is to support informal learning with the basics learned in the formal setting.

> What does education mean to you? What should it be? Education is a term which includes both formal and informal learning. One will never learn all there is to learn within the confines of the school campus, but schooling is necessary for increasing proficiency in basic skills which are needed for productivity in any career.

"Finding Satisfaction with Your Place in Society"

Question 10: What does success mean to you? The most frequent response was "finding your place in society." The second was "working hard, become a professional," and the third was "happy with what you do." An Anglo male educator viewed success as follows:

> Being able to do what you want in life, having the financial resources you re- quire to meet your needs, and I consider being able to read easily to be an im- portant need. Having the confidence to pursue strong academic interests.

Another mainstream teacher said:

> Success means reaching your goals and finding satisfaction with your place in society (and the universe).

One teacher viewed success as being directly related to education:

> Success is synonymous with education. We educate ourselves to better under- stand the issues and to develop our abilities to succeed in other areas.

An Hispanic teacher related the issue of success directly to personal identity:

> The individuation of self. Identity is not through social or economic standards of "You are what you do" but "You do that because you are who you are."

Difference in definitions of success between teachers and students were anticipated. Educators across ethnic lines equated success with education. As Manny explained before, many of his teachers defined success solely on in- strumental measures related to education and the pursuit of a college degree. For Manny, an assimilated Mexican-American youngster, success consisted in achieving the American dream through alternative ways. Becoming an entre- preneur, running his own business in the automotive field, and enjoying his occupation were for Manny forms of success not shared by his teachers.

To Carla success meant functioning in a more social and holistic way. This included helping others realize their educational aspirations and teach- ing "others what they hadn't taught her."

"The Availability of Choices"

Question 11: What do you think are the most important things for a Latino student to achieve in life? Many of the respondents gave a neutral answer to this question with such comments as "same as all other students" or "whatever they choose to do in life." The categories of responses to this question were personal (P), power/identity (PI), and community/social (CS). The majority of responses were in the first two categories: a typical power/identity (p) response related to students' personal achievements:

> The most important thing for a Latino is to achieve his or her dreams, to be able to become whatever he or she wishes to become.

Hispanic respondents often mentioned either or both power and identity in their responses as necessary ingredients for success in life.

> Everyone needs meaningful work that does not degrade the person in any way. Everyone needs power to make decisions, maintain a decent standard of living, and the opportunity to achieve those goals. Most people need the ability to properly care for a family both in the terms of time and money. Everyone needs a purpose in life.

And another said:

> The availability of choices. Foremost is empowerment. If people feel themselves empowered, there is more opportunity for choosing for wholeness. Success is not the same for all people, obviously. Why else would I need to define my own version of success? However, too many Latino students have no real choices in their lives given the constraints of powerlessness under which many of them exist.

Community/social responses indicated establishing some link with the community and exercising leadership as a measure of success. One teacher responded:

> Self-worth. To be a prosperous individual in whatever community you choose to live in. Also to give back what you take out of life.

See Table 5.3.

"They Can Be Their Own Worst Enemy"

Question 12: What obstacles do Latino students face in reaching their goals? This question evoked some of the most lengthy narratives, some strong opinions, and some very divided opinions. The primary obstacles identified by many respondents, regardless of race, were racism and discrimination, which were followed by language barriers. A variety of other obstacles were "self-concept barriers," "lack of motivation," "lack of role models," and "peer pressure."

TABLE 5.3   Number and Frequency of Responses to Question 8

	Classifications of Teacher Responses							
	Personal		Power Identity		Community Social		Total	
Ethnicity	Freq.	%	Freq.	%	Freq.	%	Freq.	%
Anglo	14	54%	7	27%	5	19%	26	100%
Latino	9	43%	12	57%	0	0%	21	100%
African American	3	60%	2	40%	0	0%	5	100%

Note. Total: $N = 33$; Anglos: $n = 20$; Latinos: $n = 10$; African Americans: $n = 3$

Although racism and discrimination were identified strongly as obstacles, many of the respondents reiterated the personal and community "pathologies" identified in earlier questions. In essence, these responses blamed students or their families and communities for the students' failures in school. For example, while I was distributing the questionnaires, an older Anglo female teacher questioned the use of "Latino" in the questions. She noted, in front of a number of her Hispanic students standing nearby, that the only Latinos she was teaching were "lower-class Mexicans." Accordingly, in her survey she noted the greatest obstacles as "ignorance and parochialism. This is true of any student—Aren't we supposed to be leading all students toward greater understanding?"

Another Anglo teacher literally did "blame the victim" but in a slightly gentler way:

> The greatest obstacles students face are themselves. They can be their own worst enemy. Pressure they place on themselves to conform to what peers are doing can cloud their focus on the future. Students need to dream. Need to prepare themselves in a role which will achieve self-sufficiency. A role that will bring them happiness. Lack of success in school is the first step toward a negative self-image.

The opinions on language as an obstacle were divided. Among the Anglo teachers, language was invariably considered a "barrier" and thus an obstacle to success:

> Latino students often face language barriers, money difficulties, and lack of role models as far as education goes. I think many of those students have wonderful role models of family and community. Latino students tend to struggle more with expressing themselves in written form and believing that their ideas mat-

ter. Many of these students struggle against peer pressures that demand that they not be "school boys" or "school girls." So we need to teach these young people that knowledge is a means to power and fulfillment.

There were stronger opinions on language issues:

> Bilingual education, when the students become locked into these programs, they are guaranteed a place in the lower levels of society. In the United States the primary language of business is English and if you cannot function in that language from 9 to 5, the opportunities are very limited. Too many students complete this program and still are unable to function in English adequately. Note: I think this study is very prejudicial. We should be working to improve the lot of all students, not just select groups. If we keep doing this, we will become a very fragmented society and this will do nothing but create more and more problems.

Opinions were also divided on matters related to curriculum. In discussing this issue, an Hispanic male administrator identified the major issues of access to curriculum:

> Today, equal access to the curriculum is one of the major obstacles for the Latino student. Another major obstacle is poverty. An over-representation of our Latinos lives in poverty and that denies them the opportunity to develop to their potential.

An Anglo teacher saw the problem as one of needing to create a better "fit" in the curriculum but in a very different way from that expressed by the Hispanic administrator:

> The obstacles are many. Latinos have to start by integrating themselves into the Anglo curriculum and have teachers teach them as well as their Anglo counterparts.

Another teacher took a different view, indicating that family attitude toward education is paramount:

> Hispanic students who have family support with positive expectations of the educational program generally have success. Any student whose family does not place education as a high priority will have to struggle through the system.

Summary and Conclusions

An holistic analysis of the teachers' responses reveals several key issues. Although there were no consistently uniform and clear divisions in the ethnic group membership of respondents across every question, there were some general patterns of responses that were associated with ethnicity, that is, in the way Latino students were perceived by their teachers and administrators.

Although acknowledging that racism and discrimination are strong factors affecting Latino students, Anglo educators tended to attribute negative pathologies to the students and their communities, blaming the students for the failures they experienced in school. Some of the pathologies that Anglos perceived addressed poor language skills, absence of role models, lack of commitment to their own education, and noninvolvement or support by family members. Hispanic and African-American respondents, on the other hand, tended to attribute student failure to community/psychological issues and political and social-structural issues as well as bureaucratic obstruction. Key issues of students not being represented in the curriculum and lack of proportional representation in the teaching force were often mentioned as part of these structural problems.

Language was cited as an issue many times in the responses. Again, there tended to be considerable division. Anglo teachers often decried the students' lack of language skills as an obvious "deficit" or "barrier." Hispanic teachers often mentioned language problems, but they also suggested that language might not be an insurmountable problem if students' language and culture were adequately represented in the curriculum.

One of the more interesting patterns was the educators' responses to Latino studies and who should teach it. Most of the Latino teachers associated Latino studies with cultural reinforcement and empowerment, a necessary ingredient, in their view, for student success. The Anglo and African-American educators sought more "bridges across cultures" in their responses, saying that such studies should either be available to all students or infused throughout the curriculum in the form of multicultural courses. Similarly, Anglo teachers saw any good teacher as capable of teaching Latino studies. Many Hispanics agreed, but they also expressed a need for equal representation in the curriculum and teaching force.

There was a similar pattern in views about role models. All groups agreed role models were essential to the development of Latino youth. Anglo teachers tended to view role models as being needed in the community and family, especially to promote the effective use of educational opportunity. Latino educators associated role models as a need in the school and in the teaching force. There seemed to be an underlying issue of control. Latinos argued for increasing their numbers whereas Anglos argued for more of a "melting-pot" approach to curriculum and ethnic studies. For Anglos, this seemed to justify the fact that they dominate faculty numbers in the school.

Generally, all the educators viewed the educational system as failing to do its job. Although they acknowledged that good teachers can make a powerful difference in a student's life, they cited social ills and a poor educational system as the causes of failure. Latinos and African Americans generally tended to see the system and society as needing to change if Latino students are to succeed. Anglos tended to view the opposite: Latino students, their communities, and their language need to change if they are to succeed. In terms of *success*, most educators appeared to define the term in relation to education and the pursuit of a college career, even when, for some, success was defined in terms of personal fulfillment and happiness. The results of this chapter serve as a basis of comparison with the students' views, presented in more detail in the following chapter.

F O R   D I S C U S S I O N

1. How could teachers work toward greater community participation in a school? Specifically in establishing a language policy for the school?

2. Schools reinforce social inequities by giving high status to registers of language not utilized in the community. How can schools change to integrate the language needs of diverse students? Provide specific examples.

3. In this chapter many educators discussed the inclusion of a Latino studies course in the school's curriculum. Imagine that as an educator you were called to design this curriculum. What components would the course have? How would you make sure that the course would meet the needs of all ethnic students represented in the school? Explain your rationale.

4. The educators in this study explained their views on who should teach Latino studies courses. What are your views on this issue?

5. In what specific ways do you see culturally compatible educators as benefiting bicultural students? What do mainstream teachers need to know before they can educate Latino children?

6. As a teacher or school administrator, what steps would you take to change or reform school policies that you believe are detrimental to students' success?

7. Is language testing useful? How frequently should it be carried out? What should the objectives be? Who should do the testing?

8. Throughout the book you heard the voices of students and educators describing good and mediocre bilingual programs. Think of your school, its realities, and its students' needs. What would be the characteristics of a good bilingual program for your school?

CHAPTER

6

Toward a Self-Definition of Success

Two dominant themes emerged from the interviews with Carla and Manny presented in earlier chapters. The first is that of the hidden curriculum of the school, specifically, the schools and their respective politics of language, teacher–student interactions, the mechanisms of discipline, the presentation of school knowledge, and interracial conflicts. The second dominant theme has to do with issues of resistance and identity. This chapter explores these pervasive themes as they relate to the school experiences of Carla and Manny, the Latino students in this study. Then it compares and contrasts the themes in the students' narratives with the educators' responses derived from the analysis of questionnaires.

A common perception among public school educators and the public in general is that minority students drop out of school because of personal deficiencies, language difficulties, poverty, and many other perceived culturally ingrained pathologies. Because of the concentration on the students and their families as the problem, few serious actions have been taken to investigate the school's responsibility related to the dropout phenomenon. Thus, the statistics continue to rise as one of every three Latino students abandons his or her education. The two at-risk Latino students interviewed in this study provided considerable evidence that the characteristic "culture" of the school and the teacher–student interactions in the classroom contributed to the problem. As some studies have reported (Davidson, 1996; Fine, 1991), minority youth who have dropped out of school have been found to be highly critical of the school. They are well aware of the wide gaps between their academic learning and their lived experiences.

Manny and Carla in this study consistently voiced their opinions not only on the lack of connection between their life experiences and the school curricula but also on their negative interactions with school authorities and teachers, the school policies, the teacher and administrative insensitivity to students' emerging adult roles, and the lack of respect for their language and identity. For example, Manny summed it best when he said, "I wonder why we act like kids? We get treated like kids. . . . He wrote me a referral for standing up to throw a piece of paper in the trash." Manny was frequently punished for

117

voicing his opposition to what he considered infantile school procedures not appropriate in a high school environment.

Both interviews often provided evidence on the punishments these students received in school. In fact, the strict disciplinary policies exacerbated the very problems the school was intending to curtail. In the following section, overt and covert school procedures that affect both immigrant and American-born Latinos are examined. The nature of the commonalities are highlighted between Carla, the immigrant student, and Manny, the American-born Latino, in their relationships with the school system.

The Politics of Language

Schools are political domains and are linked to power and control within the dominant society. They are also agents of socialization in which formal pedagogy as well as the informal hidden curriculum reflect the beliefs of the dominant society (Giroux, 1983). Throughout the interview process, both Carla and Manny maintained a firm belief that their language was not part of the school curriculum. They entered their schools with a richness of cultural and linguistic competencies. Their bicultural homes were sources of cultural and cognitive resources or "funds of knowledge" (Moll, Amanti, Neff, & Gonzalez, 1992) that constituted for these students "sets of meanings, qualities of styles, modes of thinking" (Bordieu & Passeron, 1977, p. 30).

These students brought to the school a valid language and culture that were not utilized but rejected by the school's assimilationist orientation. Carla experienced these assimilationist pressures most directly when her teachers outwardly confronted her for speaking Spanish with such reprimands as "This is America and here you speak English." Throughout American history, the drive for Anglo-American hegemony has forced the elimination of non-English languages and cultures. Since the 1980s and 1990s the orientation has been to anglicize large numbers of Mexicans. The underlying purpose of these activities seem not to be the academic well-being of Latino students but, rather, according to Hernandez-Chavez (1995), "the disintegration of language minority cultures in American society in order to eliminate the possibility of separatist tendencies" (p. 157). Carla reported:

> They would call my parents to tell them I didn't want to speak English. . . . I didn't like their pushy ways.

A language is not only a means of communication, but it is also a very personal symbol for the individual. As Fishman (1995) noted, "A language is a precious marker of cultural belonging, behavior and identity" (p. 51). Carla's teachers' constant pressure to reject and replace her language not only affected her self-esteem but also made her believe that the school considered both her culture and language inferior. At the same time, the effect these language restrictions had upon Carla's parents was detrimental. Her parents' involvement in the academic activities of the school and their communication with Carla's teachers and school authorities were severely inhibited by the school's language restrictions. The school's exclusion of Carla's parents from participation in the school because of their limited English proficiency resulted in reinforcing an inferiority complex. Even their interaction with Carla in Spanish at home was regarded by Carla's teachers as contributing to her academic difficulties. Carla reported:

> The teachers wanted me to speak English at home, watch TV in English. I felt ridiculous talking in English with people that spoke Spanish.

As a consequence of the promotion of the English language as the exclusive medium of communication in the schools, Spanish language competency has diminished even among recent immigrant students. Pressed by the harmful monolingual enforcement in the schools and the subtractive rapid transitional programs, Latino students are shifting dramatically to English (Hernandez-Chavez, 1978). It comes as no surprise that some Mexican-American families affected by the imposition of the schools and, ignoring the benefits of bilingualism, often agree with the school's English-only programs.

Manny's parents, as many other families in Arizona, learned well the message that their language was not welcome at school. As a result, they made a conscious decision to raise Manny as a monolingual English speaker. Few people have explored in depth the scope of losses when the family language is annihilated: the socio-cultural integration of the generations, the secure sense of identity as well as the consciousness of an identity, and, more importantly, the sense of collective worth (Fishman, 1995). The psycho-social consequences for an individual and his community are devastating.

Manny reported during our interviews that because his identity as a Chicano was not affirmed he felt strongly devalued. He believed that Chicanos at school not only did not have a right to the language closest to their identity, but they also did not have a "voice" (Ruiz, 1991).

Manny prided himself on being a Chicano. As such, he expressed many beliefs of the working-class Mexican. His forms of speech, dress, style, and socializing were viewed by his teachers as essentially tacky, vulgar, or linguistically unsophisticated. His teachers judged his version of English and his academic efforts from their own vantage point. At times he felt that they considered his being and identity culturally inferior. Manny reported that Chicano English, which he considered his "natural" language, was not accepted in school projects and assignments:

On one occasion I presented a paper that had to do with racism at school. But the teacher put restrictions on the language I could use in the paper. I couldn't use students' language. I had to change all the paper.

Bourdieu and Passeron (1977) coined the term *cultural capital* to refer to the knowledge, skills, and cultural background transferred from one generation to the next. Cultural capital includes ways of talking, values, and socializing modes, which Manny made reference to. As McLaren (1989) stated, "Schools generally affirm and reward students who exhibit the elaborately coded middle-class speech while disconfirming and devaluing students who use restricted working class coded speech" (p. 191).

Manny's voice seems to testify that at school his cultural capital was devalued because his identity and culture occupied a subordinate class position. Manny's observations that the school curriculum did not relate to the realities of the community, such as the school's failure to recognize "Chicano English or Spanglish" usage among the school's students, is a good example of this. Both of these students' narratives reflect the active promotion of an assimilationist school orientation that viewed linguistic differences as "cultural deficiencies." This orientation seemed to exist whether or not it was applied to Carla, the immigrant and student, or Manny, the American-born caste-like analytic typology. Further, the relationship between both students and the school system exhibited more commonalties than differences. Carla's and Manny's testimonies are a reflection of the power relations that exist within the broader society. At the same time, their interactions with certain educators reflect dynamics typical of dominant–subordinate group relations.

Teacher–Student Interactions

A second area in which the influence of the dominant culture is revealed resides within the microinteractions among teacher and students in school. For Manny and Carla, their teachers were at the heart of their schooling experience. They evaluated much of the worth of their experience on the basis of interactions with their teachers. Some researchers (Weis, 1985) have concluded that teacher–student relationships are a key variable in students' feelings about schools. Manny and Carla felt that a teacher should be a friend rather than just a facilitator of learning. They perceived that if the school environment were an extension of a family network, students would not be inclined to drop out. For Carla, most of her teachers, with the exception of two mentors during her senior year, were people who did not care for their students. The image of teachers who took roll, lectured at a fast pace, and quickly left the room contrasted sharply with her teachers in Mexico who were caring and a part of her extended family. By the same token, for Manny, a good teacher was someone who took personal responsibility for students' learning as parents would for the learning of their children. Most of Carla's and Manny's teachers in high school, who were overwhelmed by crowded classrooms, emphasized greater self-reliance and initiative. This emphasis created the impression that their teachers "did not care," leaving the students feeling frustrated in their attempts to function in a learning environment without the reciprocal responsibility that had sustained them in the past. Both students perceived most teachers as being aloof and unconcerned about an individual student's problems or learning needs. As Carla said:

> Here most teachers are always in a hurry, they only have time to make money not to talk to us. You enter the class, the teacher lectures, and you are out.

Corroborating Carla's ideal on teachers, Manny distinguished between the "bull_____rs" and the "straightforward" teachers. For Manny, good teachers were those who gave him choices on how to learn and who did not unnecessarily show their power and control.

The impact of teacher racism and stereotyping as complex factors working against Latino students was another constant and recurrent finding in this study. According to Cummins (1989), teachers have the means to convey subtle messages to students regarding the value of their language and culture. Both students in this study, however, reported not subtle but overt messages from teachers and administrators regarding their culture and language. As the data suggest, Carla, the immigrant student, did not drop out of school because of her limited English skills, her placement in a mediocre transitional program, or lack of parental support. As she reported, her two-year separation from school came about as a direct result of teacher racism and verbal harassment on the part of school authorities. As Carla stated:

> I left the school because I came to the conclusion that there was too much racism in that school. What a coincidence that only Mexicans would drop out.

Cummins (1997) stated that microinteractions between educators and students are never neutral. His framework points out that these interactions either promote collaborative relations of power or reinforce coercive power relations. "Human relationships enacted in the interactions between educators and students are embedded within a matrix of historical and current power relations between groups in the wider society" (p. 425). The historical power relations between Mexican Americans and the majority culture are reflected in Manny's and Carla's school experiences. The schooling experience of Manny, the caste-like student, reflected the same salience on ethnicity as in Carla's story. Both students viewed themselves as being outside the full participation of society's culture because of their Latino heritage. Manny said:

Here, it's just you're Mexican. They treat you the same way as the other Mexicans over there.

Both students viewed themselves as marginal in relationship to the dominant society. Both expressed a desire for more acceptance of Latinos in society. They did not express any desire to exchange their identity for another. Their ideal was equal membership and having the same options as any other mainstream student enjoys. In addition, Carla and Many lived in constant awareness and fear of being treated stereotypically as inferior Mexicans. Their sense of being stereotyped was acquired through the media, but most particularly through their negative experiences with both Latino and non-Latino educators. Manny and Carla stated:

They thought I was a drug dealer because of my nice car and pager. (Manny)

The teacher would say things like, "Wetbacks, the *Migra* is coming to get you." He would embarrass us. (Carla)

Intimidation played an important role in the treatment of Latino students. Knowing that their life experiences were different from those of non-Latino students kept both Carla and Manny from becoming actively involved in school. In fact, both students revealed during interviews that they did not take part during or after school in any of the enrichment activities programmed by the school.

Addressing the stereotype was an important motivating factor for pursuing education for these students. Because these students perceived that an aspect of stereotyping had to do with school achievement, they felt a personal and moral obligation to prove themselves and help break the stereotypes. As Manny summarized:

One day I got so tired of their suspicious attitudes I said to myself, "OK, you think I'm a drug dealer? That's the image I'm going to give you . . . but I'm graduating. How many drug dealers graduate?

Succeeding and graduating from high school were very symbolic for these students in terms of feeling a sense of equality with other racially diverse students. Graduating from school was also a way of satisfying the aspirations that their parents and extended family had placed upon them. Even when both Manny and Carla openly demonstrated an oppositional identity, they accomplished their goal of high school graduation.

Several international studies (Cummins, 1997; Gillborn, 1997; Van Zanten, 1997) have added evidence to the role of teacher racism and school-based factors in perpetuating inequalities and impeding the success of ethnic minority students in school. As this study seems to suggest, both Latino students, Carla and Manny did not differ in their perceptions of American society but recognized and experienced the same racist societal constraints. The present economic and social status of Latino-origin peoples in the United States and their ongoing struggle to assert their identities and language have influenced in an expected manner classroom and school conflicts. As the testimonies of Carla and Manny revealed, their interactions with educators and school authorities were influenced by the status of their language and culture in the society. This, in turn, influenced their teachers' expectations of their academic achievement.

The implication of the present study relates to the lack of belonging expressed by the students. First, Manny's and Carla's lack of personal contact with some of their teachers made them feel out of place, isolated, and unwelcome. They verbalized their reactions to their teachers' lack of care. Second, Carla and Manny perceived that their academic development took place in an environment in which Latinos are stereotyped and perceived negatively. Third, both students considered education as a way to reduce their marginality and society's stereotyping. Overall, the students were well aware of the standards used by others to judge them. The descriptions these students provided of themselves as Latinos in this society indicated the depth of sensitivity minority students have acquired and the impact that negative interactions have exerted on their lives.

Mechanisms of Discipline

Both students frequently criticized school policies on student class behavior, discipline, and punctuality. Disciplinary punishments, such as being required to remain standing and to stare at a wall for a full hour for being late, made Manny feel that he was considered irresponsible and untrustworthy. He said, "Those punishments didn't teach me anything. They were a waste of time."

School policies that ban students from wearing particular types of clothing in an attempt to control gang activity were also successful in communicating adult's ideas on the possibility of a dominant conceptualization of "deviance" among Latinos in school. Bowles and Gintis (1976) illustrated how since its conception, the public school system's role has been that of reproducing conditions of dominance and subordinacy of status groups in accordance with the demands of a capitalist economy. According to Bowles and Gintis, in the United States the public school system has been seen as a method of "disciplining children in the interest of producing a properly subordinate adult population. . . . The theme of social control pervades educational thought and policy" (p. 37).

Work within Manny's and Carla's classrooms in which the majority of students were of Latino heritage consisted of following strict rules. Students in these classrooms were not allowed to leave their seats without the teacher's authorization; they completed classroom work on their own; and they spoke only when they received the teacher's approval. Thus, the hidden curriculum of these classrooms was to form the personality and dispositional traits that would later be required in the labor market. Very often the rigidity of the procedures resulted in disciplinary referrals that created school suspensions or physical separation from the classroom. Such punishments, as Manny reported, were academically counterproductive because the frequent interruptions of instruction left students unable to catch up with school work. Manny strongly criticized the lengthy and slow bureaucratic procedures students have to follow in order to comply with school rules. The rigorous and unimaginative attempts to enforce rules and correct behavior very often exacerbated the problems and added new ones. The school's lack of alternative approaches to discipline, other than negative punishments, worked to further define adolescents as either the successful or deviants (Davidson, 1996).

Data gathered from Manny's school profile for the 1996–1997 school year revealed that there were 440 school suspensions out of 1,568 students enrolled. Out of this total enrollment, 89.3% were of Latino origin (Tangerine Unified School District, 1996–1997). Yet, in a suburban middle-class high school in the same district there were only 127 suspensions that same year. This school had a very similar school enrollment as Manny's school, 1,518 students, of which only 13% were ethnic minorities. The numbers reveal that given two schools with almost the same student enrollment, the urban institution with a majority Latino population had almost four times the number of suspensions than the majority White school.

Using this statistical evidence, we can conclude that the more ethnically diverse the school, the more differentially noticeable the enforcement of disciplinary procedures. The proliferation of cultural conflicts between educators and students was not only a phenomenon identifiable in urban institutions. As Carla explained in an earlier chapter, during the years she attended a rural high school, she felt that disciplinary procedures were even stricter than in urban settings. Mexican immigrant students were severely reprimanded and punished for not speaking in English, for failing to be punctual, and for attempting to work in a collaborative manner with their classroom peers.

It was precisely because of a tardy referral and an unfortunate encounter with the school principal that Carla decided not to return to school. School authorities following traditional concepts of discipline appeared inflexible to Carla. This inflexibility exacerbated the language barrier between school authorities and Mexican immigrant students. Hence, the removal of Latinos from the schools' rolls became a semi-organized daily occurrence embedded in cultural insensitivity and conflict.

In sum, both Manny and Carla seemed to agree that both disciplinary policies and school administrative practices varied in their treatment, specifically in relationship to Latinos. They felt that these policies were more selectively enforced when Latino students were concerned. As Manny and Carla reported in previous chapters, there is an urgent need for a just and neutral administration of schools.

Their voices seem to tell us that our schools should be run by people who are sensitive to the cultural differences and needs of Latino youth. As Manny reported earlier, at school he felt that each school administrator advocated for students of his or her own ethnic background. Manny's school principal, an African American, openly demonstrated her advocacy and protection of African-American students while the school majority composed of Latinos felt as outsiders. School district documents seem to corroborate Manny's and Carla's argument that Latinos are overwhelmingly over-represented in school suspensions.

A breakdown of district ethnic data by number of suspensions indicates that in Manny's high school (in which the principal was an African American) only one African-American student was suspended in 1996, whereas, the number of Latinos suspended for the same length of time was 102 students (Tangerine Unified School District, 1996–1997). It is the responsibility of sensitive and empowered educators as well as the school community in general to begin questioning the nature of this escalating rate of suspensions and school expulsions.

Through a close examination of the policies and practices described above, we can reveal the layers of systemic and racially predicted school failure. We can understand the psychological impact that the use of punishments and other control devices have on minority students. We can see how Latinos are trained to accept their lower places at the bottom of the class economy through the encouragement of docility and conformity to extreme rules and authority.

School Classroom Instruction

Another area in which the imprint of the hidden curriculum and the dominant culture was visible in the lives of Carla and Manny was in the teachers' selection and presentation of school knowledge. Critical theory acknowledges that schools and their dominant ideology shape students though standardized learning situations, rules of conduct, classroom organization, teaching and learning styles, and the total physical and instructional environment. As McLaren (1989) stated:

> The hidden curriculum deals with the tacit ways in which knowledge is constructed. It is part of the bureaucratic and managerial press of the school—the combined forces by which students are induced to comply with dominant ideologies. (p. 184)

For Carla and Manny, the hidden curriculum was also reflected in the basic and remedial programs in which they were placed. Content in these classes was characterized by a mechanical presentation of knowledge, in teacher-centered instructional approaches, in the superficial treatment of Latino students' culture and identity in the curriculum, in the way administrators disempowered Carla's and Manny's few caring minority teachers who advocated for their students, in the low expectations their teachers held about their academic possibilities, and in the school's dismantling classes and programs that were empowering and engaging to students at school.

Carla revealed to us that during her first semester in college she began to learn how to write an essay. Her instructors offered her remedial lessons independently and were puzzled to learn of the little preparation she received at school. Carla felt that school and the watered-down curriculum she followed did not prepare her for college. She was fully aware of the inequalities that existed between "honors" classes designed for her Anglo peers and the sheltered and remedial bilingual classes she was placed in. Her school assignments normally consisted of copying answers she would find in textbooks. Carla was racially segregated in mediocre programs called "bilingual" in which it was obvious that her teachers had not received proper training and had very low expectations for their Latino students.

For Manny, school instruction was not much different. During our interviews he revealed that real learning of content was minimal. His high school, which had the lowest standardized test scores in the district, reflected the poor teaching and mechanization of learning. For him, school was a mechanical game that consisted of doing only what was necessary to pass the classes, not learning the content. As in the case of Carla, Manny's assignments consisted, for the most part, in mechanically answering questions from textbooks. These students' testimonies indicated that the way knowledge was presented at school prepared them only to maintain their subordinate status and class positions in the wider society. Some of the school's mechanisms of social reproduction include what Freire (1970) defined as "banking" transmission of knowledge, or in Manny's words, "school as the killer of your natural curiosity." As Freire (1981) stated, "Education is the practice of freedom not the act of depositing reports or facts in the educatee . . . " (p. 149).

Carla and Manny reported that, for the most part, their teachers enjoyed lecturing from textbooks and, according to Carla, "talking to themselves." They both felt that learning took place on a few occasions when teachers let them choose the learning style and method most suited for them. They strongly criticized school counselors who were unavailable when they needed them. Both students reported that there was a two- to three-week waiting period before a student could see a counselor. Carla said that while she was an office aide during her senior year she did have more access to counselors and could sign up for classes. Manny reported that even after meeting with counselors, he found that the classes he selected were booked and unavailable. However, he normally found space in vocationally oriented courses.

Their strongest criticisms came as a result of their awareness that the school curricula did not speak of or to their culture and identity. They said that the few minority teachers who attempted to diversify the curriculum were soon discharged and disempowered. Manny talked about the superficial treatment of Native Americans and Hispanics in his history classes; their stories were often twisted and reduced to a brief mention in one-year history courses. For example, Carla mentioned Cinco de Mayo, the only ethnic celebration allowed but under the condition that it be attended only by Latino students. Manny said there was only one class he loved at school. His Literature of the Southwest class taught him about his Mexican background. Contradictorily, given the success of the class among Chicano students, it was rapidly removed from the school curriculum. The principal removed the class from the curriculum at the same time that the Latino student school organization MECHA (Mexican Chicano Association) was dismantled. Manny stated:

> Mr. Galvan—that teacher was the greatest. He taught us about Mexicans, where we came from. It was the only class I loved.

Manny enjoyed Mr. Galvan's class because he started to appreciate himself and his culture. Empowerment is gained from knowledge that honors one's history, language, and cultural traditions. But as McLaren (1989) added:

> Empowerment also refers to the process by which students learn to question and selectively appropriate those aspects of the dominant culture that will provide them with the basis for defining and transforming rather than merely serving the wider social order. (p. 186)

As Carla and Manny revealed in the interviews, there were no classes they remembered that empowered their sense of collective identity and belonging. Their classes did not provide them with opportunities to establish dialogue and discuss the problems that affected them and their communities. Their teachers, and especially the school administration, controlled and selected knowledge and the way to present it. Minority students in large urban schools like Carla and Manny attended had no say in the selection of what or how they wanted to learn. As Giroux (1992) denounced:

> Whenever power and knowledge come together politics not only functions to position people differently with respect to the access of wealth and power, but it also provides the conditions for the production and acquisition of learning. (p. 162)

In terms of ways of learning, both Carla and Manny indicated preference for mutual problem solving and team effort in which each member of a
group contributed in his or her own way to the acquisition of knowledge.
They generally disliked situations in which they did not feel personally involved. They expressed a preference for interactive and cooperative learning
situations that are extant within Latino culture. Such opportunities were few
for them at school. For the most part, their teachers preferred the lecture style
and did not trust that real learning would take place if students worked co-
operatively. When Manny and Carla relied on their peers for help, their teachers gave them disciplinary referrals. Individual effort was rewarded and
emphasized. Manny favored classes that taught him something practical
based on cooperative effort. Courses such as graphic arts, media arts, or printing left him the feeling that he "produced" something on his own, and was in
control of his own learning. Only in these vocational classes did Manny feel
that both teacher and students worked together toward a common goal.

Both Manny and Carla frequently expressed their dissatisfaction with the
lack of connection of school knowledge to the real world. The development of
students' critical consciousness and thinking was not a priority in Manny's and
Carla's urban institutions whose mission and ideology, as seen through these
students' voices, were to assimilate and preserve the status quo. Some of the
students' most meaningful statements are presented below in their words:

> I wasn't able to produce things. (Manny)
> Teachers don't give you options. (Carla)
> It's 1996—there's a lot more than Whites out here. (Manny)
> They have to be more human. (Carla)
> There's no room to think. (Manny)

Interracial Conflict

An atmosphere of peace, social harmony, and respect that should exist in an
educational institution in which various ethnic groups coexist was of deep concern to both students in this study. Carla and Manny described with genuine
feeling the frequent occasions in which instruction was interrupted by racial
confrontations and violence. Manny talked about the omnipresence of police
cars parked near the school patio, which conveyed the impression of a prison
rather than a learning institution. He described the numbers of uniformed
monitors and school personnel equipped with radios constantly surveying the
school. School principals, he said, seemed accustomed to fights between ethnic groups that automatically resulted in the expulsions of the participants.

Carla's first impression of an urban school was the extreme racial and social segregation on the patios and hallways of her high school. The sporadic

fights between Anglos and recent Mexican immigrant students at her rural school were minimal compared to the frequent violent conflicts she witnessed during her senior year at the large urban institution. According to Carla, these conflicts often required the involvement of the local police force who would normally arrest minority students, even if they had not instigated the conflicts. After the fights, "it was hard to concentrate again on the lessons," she recalled, for the students only wanted to talk about the incidents and their causes. For Carla, the issue of an harmonious and peaceful school environment was very important. She could not understand why such persistent problems had not received more attention from the school's administration. She commented:

> If I were a school principal, the problem with the fights would be the first one I would solve. Maybe organizing activities so that we all could have friendships among races.

Carla's statements reflected a feeling of racial isolation and sense of helplessness. The school's indifference to confronting and dealing with the issues of racial tension not only indicate that urban schools are, in reality, "technically" desegregated spaces, but they also fail to foster a sense of community within the institution.

> Believe. I believe that Mountain High is not a unique school. I feel that it exemplifies what goes on in many urban desegregated high schools across the nation.

After years of research and observation in public schools, Fine, Weis, and Powell (1997) found that the existence of interactional barriers characterized by the informal practices of schooling, ideologies, and formal structures work together to resist inclusion. They proposed an "equal status" theory that says it is necessary to improve multiracial group relations by the active promotion of equal status among the different groups represented in the school.

The different status each racial group enjoyed at school was reflected in the curriculum, in internal tracking, and in the racially predicted academic achievement at Manny's and Carla's schools. These, in turn, influenced the ways students perceived school and the racial relations among groups. Schools that have difficulty creating authentic democratically accessible services and programs for *all* students foster the feelings of "us versus them" among high school youth.

The problem of truly collaborative integrated schools is beginning to draw the attention of some researchers in the field. As seen in this study, the inclusion of students and teachers of different races in the same school does not automatically create an integrated school. There is much more to explore regarding this aspect of schooling. Fine, Weis, and Powell (1997) indicated there were very few models in the United States that have created and sustained communities of difference. In order to establish authentically cooperative and harmonious institutions within multiracial settings, young people and their educators should engage in a dialogue to critique and review the meanings of *race* and *difference*.

Issues of Resistance and Identity

One of the most persuasive and influential explanations of the inequality in educational outcomes among minority groups is the voluntary versus involuntary typology proposed by Ogbu (1987). For Ogbu, voluntary minorities accept the school "achievement ideology," whereas involuntary minorities tend to view schooling as being assimilationist and their acceptance of it as a betrayal to their ethnic identity. Ogbu implied that the ideology of resistance that involuntary minorities develop contributes to their poor academic achievement and economic success because they blame failure on racial discrimination and other structural forces. The study of Carla, the voluntary student, and Manny, the involuntary student, invited an expansion of Ogbu's fixed typology that designates very distinct ideologies between voluntary and involuntary groups or individuals.

Although Manny and Carla described an educational system that was intolerant or not sympathetic to Latinos in particular, they also spoke of the opportunities they enjoyed in the system, which they earned through individual hard work and perseverance. They both considered themselves successful in the sense that they graduated from high school in spite of numerous constraints.

Manny had clear and defined goals for his future, and he did not discard the possibility of continuing his education in the near future. For him, high school restricts the possibilities of success because it is only oriented toward going to college. His most cherished goal was to run his own business and become an entrepreneur in the automotive remodeling business. He regretted that high school education did not prepare students for managerial or entrepreneurship responsibilities, dedicating itself only, in his view, toward building the language skills required for college.

Manny exhibited neither a conformist nor a deterministic identity, but he believed in his individual hard work and unlimited economic opportunities. He was determined to achieve the American dream through the social values received from his family, which included learning discipline through hard work.

As Ogbu (1987) maintained, involuntary minorities tend to be the ones who attribute their academic underachievement to racism, discrimination, and other structural obstacles. In this study, it was Carla, the voluntary student, who spoke more frequently about racist practices, prejudice, and discrimination as powerful forces that attempted to impede her high school graduation and academic advancement. Carla's strong statements about the racist practices at school and the social and ethnic segregation of students indicated that the awareness of structural constraints cannot be attributed merely to involuntary caste-like minorities.

Both students developed an ideology that combined a belief in achievement with cultural affirmation. Their voices were not conformist or resigned to assimilation but were highly critical of the ways schools deny students a voice and a place in the curriculum.

Some researchers (Gibson, 1997) also maintained that in order to succeed academically, minority students developed dual identities: an academic identity and a neighborhood identity. This duality allows them to assimilate and abandon their cultural identity in order to cope with pressures at school. The "accommodation without assimilation" that Gibson discussed did not seem to be a pattern in Carla's and Manny's schooling experiences. Both Carla and Manny consistently chose their ethnic identity over "acting White." They frequently asserted their cultural worldviews and questioned the tenets of achievement theory. Carla refused to comply with coercive practices that forced her to speak in English at all times while in school. Manny, through school assignments, researched issues of racism at school and questioned enforcement of selective disciplinary rules. Manny's distinctive dress style and Chicano speech were the symbols of his allegiance, in and outside the school, to his cultural identity. Through their choice of friendships and activities at school, both students affirmed their cultural and ideological identification, not alternating between distinct identities at school or home. Rather than developing strategies for managing an academic and a separate cultural identity, these students voiced their concerns that their Latino identities and belief systems were totally opposed to those of the school.

Both students in this study affirmed that their Latino cultural background and language were very important to them. During the interviews it appeared that their perceptions of the differences between Latinos born in the United States and those born in Mexico were minimal. They perceived that noticeable differences were only found at the linguistic level. In spite of Manny's typical Chicano ambivalence due to his insecurities when speaking in Spanish, his Mexican heritage was kept alive because of his intense involvement with his extended family. After interviewing Manny's parents and grandparents, it was obvious that cultural symbols were prevalent in the home. Carla related well to both Chicanos and native-born Mexicans and felt secure in her identity. This seemed to be an important factor in her successful transition to a new life in the United States.

Summary of the Students' Findings

Carla and Manny arrived at their high schools enthusiastic and confident in their capacity to succeed. The temporary disengagement of the students from their goals occurred over time, resulting from the effects of several dimensions of interactions discussed in this chapter. Eventually, they succeeded in achieving their goal of high school graduation as a way of satisfying the aspirations their families had placed upon them, to prove themselves of their capabilities, and, in particular, to help break society's stereotyping of Latinos. The students interacted with the meanings, patterns, and ideologies of the institution mostly at a remedial level. For the most part, they did not enjoy the benefits of the high school's challenging and thought-provoking courses that would prepare them for higher education. Both of them claimed that they had never been held to any standard in which they were required to do continuous and rigorous work of an average or high quality. Both students expected a mutuality in the teaching–learning relationship. Most of their teachers, with the few exceptions of some minority teachers, did not offer the mutuality of support students expected. Their teachers maintained a social distance and remained unfamiliar with the students' community and its reality. Consequently, Manny and Carla viewed their teachers as "not caring as much."

The students faced major life issues related to their Latin heritage, such as escaping social stereotypes and finding a place in society. Moreover, they openly displayed oppositional identities against the dominant ideology of the school. Their negative interactions with the perceived bad teachers and administrators as well as the selective and rigorous school's disciplinary policies were powerful constraints that worked against the achievement of their aspirations and the affirmation of their self-defined ethnic identities.

A major finding of this study is that both Carla and Manny thought that their schools had isolated them from critical dimensions of experience. First, they felt that having been placed in remedial programs they were alienated from the sense of achievement and accomplishment they felt when they first entered high school. Second, their sense of isolation was furthered when the few classes and programs that connected their culture and learning styles to their academic goals were removed from the school's curriculum. For Carla, academic disengagement and isolation occurred when the only successful bilingual class that helped her to acquire abstract knowledge in her native language and to succeed during her freshman year was removed from the school's curriculum. For Manny, isolation occurred when the Southwest literature class (in his words "the only class I loved"), which built his language skills through Chicano literature and through learning about his roots, was removed from the school's curriculum. Both students strongly sensed the isolation and lack of real world connectedness between the school content and the community's culture and knowledge. Third, their feelings of isolation heightened when they perceived the acting out of social and racial segregation within their urban institutions. This was reflected in the frequent and at times violent conflicts and racial tensions among students and in the school's failure to socialize and foster harmonious and cooperative relationships among students from different ethnic backgrounds.

Students' and Teachers' Findings

Generally, the majority of educators who responded to the study question-naire operated in a world of perception that is very different from that of the students in this study. Not surprisingly, though, perceptions of Latino teach-ers and administrators tended to be more in accord with those of the students interviewed. Although the generation gap could account for some of the dif-ferences, the students in this study clearly viewed the overall high school set-ting as an unfriendly environment. In attempting to achieve their goals, the students encountered bad and ineffective teaching, stereotyping, academic tracking, debilitating "school rules," and racism. Although both students had positive experiences with individual teachers, they had to adapt and learn cer-tain survival skills to succeed in school while, at the same time, striving to re-ceive an education they both considered lacking in substance and quality.

The teachers generally took the view that opportunity exists if students reach for it and persist. They tended to blame student failure on the students themselves and on the communities from which they came. The teachers claimed that much was beyond their control, including those larger social problems that are reproduced in the school and a very inhibiting bureaucracy that constrains their teaching. As a result, the teachers expressed a sense of powerlessness and a lack of voice in the decisions that affected them and their students.

The most potently charged area of disagreement between students and educators in the study was the issue of language. Educators, for the most part, cited language skills as the primary reason students fail to learn, thrive, and acquire the skills they need for their future. In response, both students, in rather cloquent terms, described school as a virtual battleground where their language was concerned. Neither felt they could use the language that was most comfortable and realistic for learning. They felt so strongly about as-saults on their language and identity via the hidden curriculum that they had to create a defiant and oppositional self in order to maintain and survive in the school environment. It seemed that the educators' obsession with language as a basic skill inhibited learning and masked a much deeper and more polit-ically charged issue of language status.

A second arena of struggle between educators and students was race and ethnic relations. The educators tended to perceive school as a model mini-society in which the races are all equal and democracy prevails. They expected all students to act the same. While the students in this study constantly re-ferred to difficulties among racial groups on campus, no teacher referred to it specifically in his or her questionnaire. They tended to deny that there are true ethnic divisions in society but instead exhorted a melting-pot ideology.

Although most agreed that ethnic studies programs have merit, they also felt that such courses should be available as elective courses for all students, not exclusively for Latinos. Opinions were divided in terms of who would teach such courses. However, most agreed that they should be taught by a qualified individual of any race and not necessarily a Latino. The students, on the other hand, perceived school authorities as suppressing programs and removing or inhibiting school employees who tried to focus on empowering students from a particular ethnic or racial point of view, especially when the students seemed to be enjoying or greatly benefiting from the class or activity. Based on the testimony of the students, it appears that instead of a melting pot, segregation and racial groupings were distinct on campus, causing the continuous undercurrent of racial tensions. Instead of ameliorating divisions and reducing tensions, the attitude and efforts of the school to promote a melting-pot homogeneity actually exacerbated the situation rather than remedied it.

The students' perception that members of their own ethnic group among the school staff practiced racism against them reveals certain dynamics that can be traced to the hidden curriculum and institutionalized racism. In their socialization as teachers, Latinos have simply learned to mirror the attitudes and policies of the school and the dominant community. However, the wounds left by these teachers appeared to be much deeper because they were inflicted by "one of us."

Many Latino teachers in this study possessed great empathy for students and could see that the problem in schools had less to do with negative characteristics of the students and their communities and more to do with social–structural problems of the larger society reproduced in the schools. Unlike their Anglo counterparts, the Latino educators tended to identify a need to change the educational system and its practices rather than changing the students. They recognized that schooling is largely owned and operated by a dominant society in interaction with subordinate populations. The one thing on which teachers and students agreed was that the schools were doing a substandard job of educating.

Concluding Statements

In sum, both Latino students entered a structured system of education intolerant of differences. In general, the school's programs were adequate for the dominant culture of the school and were considered by its gatekeepers equally adequate for Latinos. The students' bicultural status was not valued or considered an enriching foundation but a detrimental condition that delayed them in their mastery of the dominant culture and language.

The issues discussed in this chapter, such as language politics, the school's rules and policies, the presentation of school knowledge, ethnic relations, and issues of oppositional identity and resistance, all mirror the political and dominating nature of schools. At the same time, they mirror the status occupied by Latinos in the society. These broader societal constraints had clearly materialized and were manifested, as seen in this study, in the negative micro-interactions between educators and students. The wide structural societal factors combined with the school-based factors cause an ever increasing gap between education and the Latino student. Powerful constraints in the academic aspirations of minority students can and should be addressed by the schools if the educational gap between majority and minority students is to be reduced.

7 Students' Concerns and Recommendations for Educational Reform

The students' testimonies in this book raise a number of issues related to equality of outcomes in educational institutions in the United States and the "politics of success" that interferes with Latino students' educational aspirations. The data presented in Chapter 2 reported that the Latino dropout rates in 2001 (and into the twenty-first century) have remained static while college entry rates have remained low compared to other groups. Although the two students in this study graduated from high school, after having dropped out, their experiences at school illuminate why so many of their peers fail to thrive in the typical educational system in the United States.

In these two case studies, the reasons for failure became evident as students' and teachers' cultural worldviews were enacted within the context of the meanings and ideologies of an urban public high school. As these distinct worldviews interacted, there was an obvious lack of mutuality in cultural and educational expectations. At the same time, there was a lack of common educational objectives not only between the teachers and the Latino students but also among the teachers themselves. Unmet educational expectations and negative interactions with teachers and school administrators heightened the students' feelings of isolation, lack of personal worth, and the perception that high school was a waste of their time.

If schools are social constructions, it is vital that they be examined from the point of view of those most affected by those constructions: Latino students themselves. Although the small sample size and case-study approach limit the generalizations that can be drawn, the in-depth nature of this study and its authentification of student voices provide a foundation for drawing out implications and "lessons learned." The most important lesson is the students' urgent call for educational reform. This chapter addresses the effects of educational institutions as forms of cultural hegemony and domination. At the same time, it includes Manny's and Carla's recommendations for transforming the educational institution in order to enable academic and self-defined success. The students' concerns, recommendations, and beliefs are summarized under the topics of (a) administrative and school climate changes, (b) systemic school reforms, and (c) transformations in teacher–student interactions.

Administrative and School Climate Changes

The first area of concern addressed by Carla and Manny involved the schools' fabrications of rules and disciplinary measures that only exacerbated rather than corrected improper behavior. Manny and Carla argued that such forms of social control and close surveillance were not only enforced by the administration with selective care with respect to minority students, but they were also developed from a majority cultural frame of reference. For example, the inflexible enforcement of punctuality often overlooked and condemned the students' family priorities or economic restraints. The automatic sanction of students who were involved in verbal conflicts with staff or substitute teachers was perceived by Carla and Manny as unfair.

The second area of concern addressed the school's lack of alternative and positive ways to address conflicts. Carla's and Manny's frequent frictions with the school administration revealed their frustration, their sense of powerlessness, and their opposition to a system they considered unfair and counterproductive. The schools' rigid disciplinary methods, and the excessive use of in and out of school suspensions, reinforced the notion that social control can only be achieved through force and power. In her study of culturally diverse students, Davidson (1996) found that "disciplinary technologies" that exhibited power as a means of control produced the very behavior it was meant to prevent.

Both students clearly described events involving long bureaucratic procedures to sanction violators of school rules. A minimal tardy referral meant interrupting their instruction and waiting long hours in an office to see a school authority. Other times, the schools' suspension policies caused students to miss several days of school, resulting in even more alienation and distancing from school academic activities. The students stated during our interviews that school authorities needed to carefully examine the academic and psychological consequences of school rules and procedures.

Students' Recommendations

The first recommendation proposed by Manny was the creation of an inclusive disciplinary committee comprised of school authorities, teachers, students, and parents that equally represented the ethnic makeup of the school. Its purpose would be to combat the contradictions between the school's goals and the enforcement of ineffective and counterproductive policies. Manny believed that a participatory school philosophy would limit the tendencies of a few principals or teachers to favor students of their own ethnic background. He validated this suggestion as being the "democratic" process that many upper-class middle schools in the suburbs utilized in their decision-making process. This committee would mutually develop a code of conduct and examine the sanctions to impose for specific situations. This democratic process, according to Manny, would not only convey the message of a fair and culturally integrated school organization but would also diminish the abuses of power and force that created conditions for student alienation and withdrawal. Schools of the twenty-first century should move beyond the factory-like environment demanding obedience and maintaining control using coercive power. Teachers and school authorities gain the respect and trust of students when their power is both conferred by the students and constructed with the students.

Several studies on school alienation (Calabrese & Schumer, cited in Davidson, 1996), emphasized positive reforms to address discipline problems. These reforms included encouraging students to develop and implement community service projects. Since the focus was on learning rather than discipline, significant adults and mentors were available to help the students experience a sense of accomplishment, ownership, and self-worth. Nevares (1992) described a more creative and positive secondary school program in which students that fall behind due to suspensions (disciplinary violations) or exhibit poor attendance are able to catch up and make up the credits they have missed. The self-paced nature of the "Credit Plus" program allowed students to map out their own curriculum and the courses they need to catch up with their peers. Students receive incentives for good attendance and academic engagement that motivate them to discover the love of learning and personal fulfillment.

What the students in this study, in the Credit Plus program, and in other programs seem to agree upon is that schools can foster collaborative communities of learning, rather than centers of conflict, through positive discipline and supportive school–student relationships. Motivating students by coercion is not an effective way and certainly not a respectful way to achieve positive results. Guiding and mediating student behavior are more feasible approaches to working with students than controlling, manipulating, and exerting autocratic power. Teachers and school authorities' roles, according to Powell, McLaughlin, Savage & Zehm (2001), should be to mediate and negotiate rules, procedures, and social responsibilities in the classroom. The purposes of negotiation and mediation are to establish individual responsibility, self-caring, self-control, and cultural solidarity. This process involves teachers, students, and school authorities working together to solve problems and make decisions. It also involves the use of power for solidarity as "mediation consists of gaining *power with*, and not *power over others*" (p. 28). Through mediation, negotiation, shared power, and genuinely caring for students, schools can promote individual responsibility, as well as promote solidarity, collaboration, and self-empowerment.

A second recommendation proposed by the students was the implementation of an antiracist education in the school curriculum. The public school system has accepted the role of serving diverse communities; however, it has failed to foster cooperative and racially integrated schools. As this book suggests, social and harmonious academic engagement across ethnic groups was not a common practice in Manny's and Carla's schools. The large urban high schools in this study were only "technically" desegregated environments. They were notoriously separated academically and socially by color and class. The unequal status among groups of students in the schools and the individual "politics" of the school leadership created the conditions for frequent tensions and deteriorated interethnic relations. Because schools reflect the societies that support them, it is not surprising that negative interactions among ethnic groups in the schools are a reflection of the power relations within the society at large.

The educators and administrators in Manny's and Carla's schools who responded to the questionnaire in this study frequently mentioned broader societal constraints, such as discrimination and racism. However, none of them acknowledged, as the students did, the deteriorated school climate in the schools or the obvious institutionalized racism. The frequent interracial confrontations and tensions that interrupted instruction were not addressed by the educators in this study as they were in the students' testimonies.

This study reveals that educators still fear to engage in a process of dialogue in and out of their classrooms to address broader as well as internal institutional issues conducive to social and collective empowerment. As Cummins (1989) pointed out:

> Educators have uncritically, and in most cases unconsciously, accepted rather than challenged the societal discrimination that is reflected in schools. (p. 51)

The September 11 tragedy in New York City not only altered global politics around the world and threatened the increasingly fragile world peace, but it also revealed a deep crosscultural crisis manifested in our inability to coexist with those of diverse beliefs and cultural worldviews. The cultural misunderstandings and interethnic frictions common in Manny's and Carla's schools parallel the tragic events we are experiencing globally. Manny and Carla manifested the need to implement anti-racist curricula in the schools. Any participant of an urban multicultural institution brings his or her own worldview biases into the interactions and relations in the school. Education and training must continue to grow in ways that bridge cultural differences and emphasize cultural commonalities. Students and teachers together must reflect on their own cultural worldviews and beliefs when they sense there is conflict with those of others. They should be given the opportunity to engage in and outside the academic setting in activities conducive to acquiring a more realistic and less theoretical understanding of other people's beliefs and worldviews.

A third student recommendation was to redefine the roles of teachers and administrators. If we are serious about facilitating the conditions for the success of minority students, educators and administrators must redefine their roles with respect to the status of minority students and their communities. This includes, first and foremost, teacher roles. Should a teacher restrict his or her role to that of being a simple transmitter of knowledge? Should a teacher ignore a school environment in which cultural tensions and conflicts are affecting student learning? Or should he or she create the conditions for crosscultural dialogue, thereby opening opportunities for student empowerment? Most educators and respondents to this study's survey, with a few exceptions, reflected a sense of conformism and powerlessness with respect to reversing the conditions of oppressed groups and to improving the school environment. Public school teachers should not remain neutral about issues of race and ethnicity. Within large multiracial institutions as the ones documented in this study, young people must be invited to "live" democracy, that is, to discuss, voice, critique, and review the very notions of race that are so fixed, hierarchical, and widely accepted in our society. Sustaining a learning community must include both negative and positive episodes in the students' daily lives and critical interrogations on the meaning of difference.

Systemic School Reforms

As we learned from the students' testimonies, they disagreed with the educators' views on the constraints that impeded their success. Their progressive withdrawal and resistance to learning came as a result of the ethnocentrism these students perceived in the institutional setting. This form of institutionalized learning "blindness" supported an arrangement of meaning and interpretations in which victims are blamed for their shortcomings and in which they are led to believe that their failures are the result of their shortcomings and deficits. After analyzing their school experiences, the students in this study concluded that they did not meet the expectations of an educational system that judged their abilities by external measures that had very little to do with their everyday lives.

Even when Carla and Manny accomplished their goal of graduating from high school, they strongly felt that their school experience was "a big waste of time." They expressed extreme negativity about their schools and indicated a sense of having graduated severely ill-prepared for future jobs or additional educational aspirations. Both students indicated that, at most, high school should be designed only as a two-year "rite of passage" to the real world.

Students' Recommendations

The first students' recommendation for school reform calls for a more challenging, intellectually engaging, inclusive curriculum. The students' awareness of academic tracking and low expectations alienated the students and created political resistance on their part. It is clear that today middle-class values and traditions predominate in education and that in order to succeed in the system, students "must understand these values and function accordingly." Middle-class majority culture values and traditions were reflected in Manny's and Carla's schools in the curriculum, in the choice of teaching methodologies, in the choice of textbooks, and in the validation of one language over another.

In the Introduction to this book, I reminisced on my first impressions of the American educational system as I came in contact with public schools. I pointed out my perception of the immense structural differences between public schooling and college environments. Corroborating my perceptions, the students in this study described community colleges as "a different world" from that experienced in their high schools. Manny talked about a more participatory and democratic instruction in college. After graduating from high school, he enrolled at a local community college. He confided to me that he even enjoyed math, a class he had strongly disliked in high school.

Carla commented that her college instructors respected and valued her ethnic background. Her first writing assignment for an English class consisted of writing about an episode in Mexican history, which she eagerly undertook and confidently completed. For the first time, Carla related that she engaged socially and academically with students of diverse ethnic backgrounds in cooperative projects. This time her assignments were not copying answers from books but were critically analyzing and researching issues that affected her life and the society in which she lives. She mentioned that she experienced a connection between learning and her daily life in college, a connection that she had not experienced in high school.

Carla was aware of the extraordinary effort and patience her college instructors dedicated to her, given the extreme remedial condition in which she initiated her college education. This contrasted greatly with uncaring high school teachers who did not challenge her academically and who devalued her bicultural background and bilingual skills. When students are treated as if they know something and their knowledge is valued, they become motivated and energized. For the two students in this study, the very act of speaking about their schooling experiences constituted a catalyst for self-empowerment and reflection.

Carla explained that all the buildings at her high school had been rebuilt and remodeled with the exception of the "vocational" building in which the bilingual program and Spanish classes were held. This old building was in such poor condition that tiles were falling from the roof, and during the rainy season her classroom was flooded. Thus students were sent the message that their language and culture were not valued.

A second student recommendation for school reform called for reducing the frustration and powerlessness that caring and dedicated teachers experience when trying to implement positive changes in curriculum and programs and trying to address their students' needs. This parallels the teachers' survey responses that suggested that teachers recognize the wider sociopolitical problems but blame their inability to serve effectively Latino students on external factors associated with these problems. However, some educators' responses in this study placed the responsibility for the static academic progress of Latinos on the Latino communities and on the lack of students' motivation and aspirations. At the same time, their responses revealed an understanding of the excessive bureaucratic obstacles enforced by the school administration.

The teachers' responses highlighted external societal obstacles, but these are not grounds to defer educational reform. Teachers and adult authorities must join efforts to pursue a radical restructuring of public schools. Conscious of the enormous economic inequalities that still persist among diverse districts, public school educators should strive for collective action to overcome their powerlessness and fear in order to interrupt inequitable practices. A central implication of this study is the recognition that in order to create urban schools that work, educators must define their roles and their professional responsibilities in terms of curriculum transformations that educate for empowerment.

One study shows that purposeful educational reforms do work. Lucas, Henze, & Donato (1990) found that six high schools, one in Arizona and five in California, serving large populations of language minority students (where Latino students were a significant majority and Whites were the minority) exhibited attitudes and practices that seemed to promote Latino student success. They noted that these schools shared eight characteristics:

1. Value placed on students' language and culture
2. High expectations of language minority students
3. Education of language minority students a priority
4. Staff development designed to help teachers and staff to serve minority languages effectively
5. Variety of specially designed courses and programs for language minority students.
6. School's counseling program giving special attention to the needs of language minority students
7. Parents encouraged to become involved in their children's education
8. School staff sharing the strong conviction to empower language minority students through their education

A common theme in these successful schools was respect for the students' language and culture. The authors noted:

> Respect for students' languages and cultures was communicated through support programs as well as academic programs. In some schools, special programs provided tutorial and counseling assistance. Teachers and Latino students were paired in mentoring and advocacy activities, thus increasing the sense among faculty of a personal connection with the students. In 'bailes' [dances], in which they learned and performed dances from different regions of Mexico. In another, a student-run group published a monthly newspaper in Spanish. (Lucas, Henze, & Donato, 1990, p. 326)

As educators, we must listen with open hearts and minds and allow students to become architects of their own learning so that they can utilize what they learn in productive and critical ways. High school adolescents and their perceptions of the educational problems that affect them have a lot to teach us.

Teacher–Student Interactions

According to this study, one of the factors that has direct impact on the success of Latino students is the students' interactions with teachers and other school authorities. As a direct result of negative encounters with school authorities, Manny and Carla dropped out of school for a period of time.

The lack of teachers' preparedness or interest in interacting positively with diverse students, their distant and depersonalized relationships, and their failure to establish classroom conditions conducive to involvement and dialogue create conditions for student alienation and opposition. The constant stereotyping and perceptions about the capabilities of Latinos, both immigrant and American born, negatively influence student motivation to persevere and succeed.

As the survey in this study confirms, teachers direct their attention more on the weaknesses of their students rather than on their cultural and linguistic strengths and knowledge. As students experience failure and face repeated negative encounters with teachers, they develop oppositional cultural patterns and alienation. This gradual alienation augments their perceptions of school as being an illegitimate and oppressive system. Although the macroeconomic and historical determinants cited by Ogbu (1978) are difficult to reverse, the micro-interactions and school-base factors that affect minority students' motivation can be much more readily transformed. I believe that there are immediate solutions and "progressive choices" that individual educators can make in their own immediate environments to transform the context in which Latino students struggle to succeed.

Public schools are ideal arenas in which socially conscious and sensitive educators can collectively work to interrupt and change the unequal distribution of power that adversely affects them and their students. Instead of blaming the system's failure on wider historical constraints, teachers must reflect on their own images of minority students' identities. Whether Latinos or Mexican Americans represent the "involuntary" or "voluntary" minorities or whether they are recent immigrants or American-born is not the central or most important issue. Both groups' identities continue to be deemed deficient and are continuously devalued in classroom interactions. In this study, the nature of the relationship between both voluntary and involuntary groups and the dominant system seem to have the same characteristics—and consequences. The educational implications echo Cummins' (1997) assertion:

> Educator–student microinteractions must explicitly challenge the coercive power structure operating in the broader society as a necessary condition for students to succeed academically. (p. 425)

It becomes a function and an obligation of responsible educators and school counselors to take an advocacy role and to employ creative intervention strategies to solve problems. The two students in this study experienced stress and psycho-social disturbances as a result of negative encounters with school administrators and some insensitive educators. Latino students are in a stressful position in the campus social structure when they attend schools in which educators and school authorities have a predominantly monocultural worldview. Stressful negative interactions between students and teachers affect students' performance in school and their desire to learn and achieve. School authorities, and counselors in particular, cannot sit back and remain uninvolved. It becomes their responsibility to help Latino and other nonmainstream students maneuver through the institutional system, to investigate educators' uncaring attitudes, and to utilize direct intervention techniques to change behavior and perceptions.

Teachers need additional preparation in order to understand their students, their students' cultures, and the communities they serve. At the same time, school districts must make serious efforts to integrate and familiarize these educators with diverse communities in order to reduce damaging and stereotypical images of minority students. In Switzerland, teachers are required one afternoon per week to visit the homes of their students and build their knowledge of the community they serve. The purpose of these visits is to reduce the cultural distance between educators and students and to promote mutual learning and trust. Despite the enormous evidence of study upon study of the effects of classroom interactions on differential school success, schools in the United States continue to amass resources and spend energy primarily on developing alternative school programs, rigorous tracking and state-mandated testing, punitive disciplinary procedures, and intolerant language policies. If Latinos are to succeed, the cultural scene of public schools—a social environment that exists in relationship to the larger society—must be acknowledged by school personnel, carefully mediated, and improved. As Manny and Carla observed, education occurs best in environments in which students perceive themselves accepted, supported, valued, and nonthreatened.

Going back to the questions that guided this ethnography: What do Manny's and Carla's testimonies tell us about Latino students' (immigrant and American born) definitions of academic and personal success? The findings in this study seem to indicate that, upon entering high school, Latino students have high personal and academic aspirations. They want to get an education that, congruent with the reality and needs of the community in which they live, will prepare them for personal advancement and success. They not only view educational achievement as a means to attain the "American dream" but as a political act. By graduating from high school Carla and Manny wanted to show their teachers and administrators that the stereotypical views of Latinos and their negative expectations were false. Beyond this, both students indicated that academic and personal success are far easier to attain in a school environment that validates their language and ethnic identities.

Conclusion

This book adds to the growing body of research for substantial changes in the way public school institutions serve Latino students. Some educators and critics of multicultural and critical theory movement contend that social class inequities are reproduced when students fail and when their communities do not offer good modeling. In actuality, the problem lies in the imposition of dominant values and patterns and in the "politics of success" implemented from a monocultural prevailing perspective.

"Success" in social institutions—schools—is measured by the acquisition of the culture of those in power. Adolescents from middle-class homes and from dominant ethnic groups tend to perform better in school than those who represent low-income, nonmainstream groups because the school's power structure is congruent with the culture of dominant middle-class families. As Lisa Delpit stated (1995), "Children from other kinds of families operate in viable cultures but not cultures that carry the codes or rules of power" (p. 122).

The Latino students in this book not only resisted overt assimilationist curricular norms, but they opposed the hidden curriculum and the external definitions of success that ultimately interfered with their own aspirations to mobility in this society. If public schools hope to reverse the pattern of failure and attrition among Latinos, conscientious efforts must be made to prepare students to function in a multicultural and global environment. A serious commitment is needed at all institutional levels, first to recognize and value the contributions of diverse communities and, second, to manifest this recognition in a just and inclusive school curriculum and organization. Such a commitment also requires the implementation of programs that can reduce the cultural distance between teachers, their students, and communities. Only through an accurate knowledge about students and their communities will an understanding of their worldviews, learning styles, and needs emerge. Since knowledge and culture are interrelated forms of capital, public schools bear the responsibility of cultural mediation as well as education. If Latino students are to succeed, they must be guided toward knowledge of the wider society while at the same time given recognition and respect for the cultural knowledge they already possess.

BIBLIOGRAPHY

Anzaldua, G. (1999). *Borderlands la frontera: The new mestiza.* San Francisco, CA: Aunt Lute Books.

Aparicio, F. R. (2000). Of Spanish dispossessed. In R. Gonzalez and I. Melis (eds.), *Language ideologies: Critical perspectives on the official English movement* (pp. 248–275). Mahwah, NJ: Lawrence Erlbaum Associates.

Arizona Department of Education. *Dropout Rate Study 1999–2000.* http://www.ade.az.us/researchpolicy [2001, June 14].

Bodfield, R. (2000, December 3). Proposition 203 vote shows a racial split. *The Arizona Daily Star,* p. A8.

Bordieu, P., and Passeron, J. C. (1977). *Reproduction in education, society and culture.* Beverly Hills, CA: Sage.

Bowles, S., and Gintis, H. (1976). *Schooling in capitalist America.* New York: Basic Books.

Chase, B. (2000, March). Editorial comments. *NEA Today,* p. 5.

Collier, V. (1992). A synthesis of studies examining long-term language-minority student data on academic achievement. *Bilingual Research Journal, 16*(1–2), 187–212.

Corson, D. (1999). *Language policy in schools: A resource for teachers and administrators.* Mahwah, NJ: Lawrence Erlbaum Associates.

Crawford, J. (1992). *Hold your tongue: Bilingualism and the politics of English only.* New York: Addison-Wesley.

Crawford, J. (2000). *At war with diversity.* Clevedon, England: Multilingual Matters.

Cummins, J. (1989). *Empowering minority students.* Ontario, CA: California Association for Bilingual Education.

Cummins, J. (1996). *Negotiating identities: Education for empowerment in a diverse society.* Ontario, CA: California Association for Bilingual Education.

Cummins, J. (1997). Minority status and schooling in Canada. *Anthropology and Educational Quarterly, 28*(3), 411–429.

Cummins, J. (2000). *Language, power and pedagogy: Bilingual children in the crossfire.* Clevedon, England: Multilingual Matters.

Darder, A. (1991). *Culture and power in the classroom: A critical foundation for bilingual education.* South Hadley, MA: Bergin & Garvey.

Davidson, A. L. (1996). *Making and molding identity in schools: Student narratives on race, gender and academic engagement.* Albany, NY: State University of New York Press.

Delpit, L. (1995). *Other people's children: Cultural conflict in the classrooms.* New York: The New Press.

Deutsch, M., Bloom, R. D., Brown, B. R., Deutsch, C. P., Goldstein, L. S., John, V. P., Katz, P. A., Levinson, A., Peisach, E. C., and Whiteman, M. (1967). *The disadvantaged child.* New York: Basic Books.

Deyhle, D. (1995). Navajo youth and Anglo racism: Cultural integrity and resistance. *Harvard Educational Review, 65*(1), 403–444.

Durand, J., and Massey, D. S. (1992). *Mexican migration to the United States: A critical review. Latin American Research Review, 27*(2), 3–42.

Fine, M. (1991). *Framing dropouts: Notes on the politics of an urban public high school.* Albany, NY: State University of New York Press.

Fine, M., Weis, L., and Powell, L. C. (1997, Summer). Communities of difference: A critical look at desegregated spaces created for and by youth. *Harvard Educational Review, 67*(2), 236–251.

Finn, C. (1987, Spring). The high school dropout puzzle. *The Public Interest,* pp. 3–22.

Fishman, J. (1995). On the limits of ethnolinguistic democracy. In T. Skutnabb-Kangas and R. Phillipson (eds.), *Linguistic human rights: Overcoming linguistic discrimination* (pp. 49–61). Berlin, NY: Mouton de Gruyter.

Foley, D. E. (1991). Reconsidering anthropological explanations of ethnic school failure. *Anthropology and Education Quarterly, 22*(1), 60–83.

Freire, P. (1970). *Pedagogy of the oppressed.* New York: Random House.

Freire, P. (1981). *Education for critical consciousness.* New York: Continuum Publishing.

Freire, P., and Macedo, D. (1987). *Literacy: Reading the word and the world.* South Hadley, MA: Bergin & Garvey.

Gibson, M. A. (1997). Exploring and explaining the variability: Cross national perspectives on the school performance of minority students. *Anthropology and Education Quarterly, 28*(3), 318–329.

Gillborn, D. (1997). Ethnicity and educational performance in the United Kingdom: Racism, ethnicity, and variability in achievement. *Anthropology and Education Quarterly, 28*(3), 375–393.

Giroux, H. A. (1983). *Theory of resistance in education: A pedagogy for the opposition.* New York: Bergen & Garvey.

Giroux, H. A. (1988). Literacy and the pedagogy of voice and political empowerment. *Educational Theory, 38*(2), 61–75.

Giroux, H. A. (1992). *Border crossing: Cultural workers and the politics of education.* London: Rutledge.

Gonzalez, R., and Melis, I. (2000). *Language ideologies: Critical perspectives on the official English movement.* Mahwah, NJ: Lawrence Erlbaum Associates.

Hammersley, M., and Atkinson, P. (1983). *Ethnography: Principles in practice.* London: Rutledge.

Hernandez-Chavez, E. (1978). Language maintenance, bilingual education, and philosophies of bilingualism in the United States. In J. E. Alatis (ed.), *Georgetown University round table on languages and linguistics.* Washington, DC: Georgetown University Press.

Hernandez-Chavez, E. (1995). Language policy in the United States: A history of cultural genocide. In T. Skutnabb-Kangas and R. Phillipson (eds.), *Linguistics human rights: Overcoming linguistic discrimination* (pp. 49–61). Berlin, NY: Mouton de Gruyter.

Hodgkinson, H. L. (1996). *Arizona education—birth to graduate school: An exploration into Arizona educational demographics* (A working conference paper prepared for the Arizona Minority Education Policy Analysis Center). Tucson, AZ: Pima Community College.

Hodgkinson, H. L. (1999). The Arizona reality. *The School Administrator, 56*(11), 13–14.

Kominsky, R. (1990). Estimating the national high school dropout rate. *Demography, 27*(1), 303–320.

Kozol, J. (1992). *Savage inequalities: Children in American schools.* New York: Harper Perennial.

Krashen, S. (1991, Spring). *Bilingual education: A focus on current research.* (Occasional papers in bilingual education, Number 3). Washington, DC: National Clearinghouse for Bilingual Education.

Krashen, S. (1998). Heritage language development: Some practical arguments. In S. Krashen, L. Tse, and J. McQuillan (eds.), *Heritage language development* (pp. 3–13). Culver City, CA: Language Education Associates.

Krashen, S. (1999). *Condemned without a trial: Bogus arguments against bilingual education.* Portsmouth, NH: Heinemann.

Kunisawa, B. N. (1988). A nation in crisis: The dropout dilemma. *NEA Today, 6*(6), 61–65.

Lucas, T., Henze, R., and Donato, R. (1990). Promoting the success of Latino language-minority students: An exploratory study of six high schools. *Harvard Educational Review, 60*(3), 315–337.

Macedo, D., and Bartolome, L. (1998). In Y. Zou and E. Trueba (eds.), *Ethnic identity and power: Cultural contexts of political action in school and society.* Albany, NY: State University of New York Press.

McCarty, T. L., Wallace, S., Lynch, R. H., and Benally, A. (1991). Classroom inquiry and Navajo learning styles: A call for reassessment. *Anthropology and Education Quarterly, 22*(1), 42–59.

McLaren, P. (1989). *Life in schools: An introduction to critical pedagogy in the foundations of education.* White Plains, NY: Longman.

McLaren, P. (1995). *Critical pedagogy and predatory culture: Oppositional politics in a postmodern era.* New York: Routledge.

McLaren, P. (1998). *Afterword: Ya Basta!.* In Y. Zou and E. Trueba (eds.), *Ethnic identity and power: Cultural contexts of political action in school and society* (pp. 411–431). Albany, NY: State University of New York Press.

Mehan, H., Hubbard, L., and Villanueva, I. (1994). Forming academic identities: Accommodation without assimilation. *Anthropology and Education Quarterly, 25*(2), 91–115.

Merriam, S. B. (1988). *Case study research in education: A qualitative approach.* San Francisco: Jossey Bass.

Moll, L., Amanti, D., Neff, D., and Gonzalez, N. (1992). Funds of knowledge for teaching: Using a qualitative approach to connect homes and classrooms. *Theory into Practice, 31*(1), 133–139.

National Center for Education Statistics. (2001). *The condition of education report November 2001* (NCES 2002–114). Washington, DC: U.S. Department of Education, Office of Educational Research and Improvement.

National Center for Education Statistics. (2001, November). *Dropout rates in the United States* (Statistical Analysis Report, NCES 2002–114). Washington, DC: U.S. Department of Education, Office of Educational Research and Improvement.

National Clearinghouse for Bilingual Education (NCBE Newsline Bulletin). (2001, June 12). [Online]. *Proposition 203 in Arizona: Educational repercussions in Southern Arizona.* Washington, DC: George Washington University. http://www.ncbe.gwu.edu/newsline [2001, June 14].

National Education Association. *Wanted: Diverse & excellent educators.* [Online]. National Education Association. <http://www.nea.org/teaching/Santana.html> [2001, September 5].

Nevares, L. (1992). Credit where credit is due. *The Executive Educator, 14*(12), 50–54.

Nieto, S. (1992). *Affirming diversity: The sociopolitical context of multicultural education.* White Plains, NY: Longman Publishers.

Oakes, J. (1985). *Keeping track: How schools structure equality.* New Haven: Yale University Press.

Ogbu, J. (1978). *Minority education and caste.* New York: Academic Press.

Ogbu, J. (1983) Minority education and schooling in plural societies. *Comparative Education Review, 27*(2), 168–190.

Ogbu, J. (1985). A cultural ecology of competence among inner-city Blacks. In M. B. Spencer, G. C. Brookins, and W. R. Allen (eds.), *Beginnings: The social and affective development of Black children* (pp. 45–66). Mahwah, NJ: Lawrence Erlbaum Associates.

Ogbu, J. (1987). Variability in minority school performance: A problem in search of an explanation. *Anthropology and Education Quarterly, 18*(4), 312–334.

Ogbu, J. (1995). Understanding cultural diversity and learning. In J. A. Banks and C. A. Banks (eds.), *Handbook of research in multicultural education* (pp. 582–593). New York: MacMillan.

Persell, C. H. (1977). *Education and inequality: The roots and results of stratification in America's schools.* New York: Free Press.

Powell, R. R., McLaughlin, J. H., Savage, T., and Zehm, S. (2001). *Classroom Management: Perspectives on the social curriculum.* Upper Saddle River, NJ: Prentice Hall.

Ramirez, J. D., Yuen, S. D., and Ramey, D. R. (1991). *Executive summary: Final report: Longitudinal study of structured English immersion strategy, early-exit and late-exit transitional bilingual education programs for language-minority children* (Contract N. 300-87-0156). Washington, DC: U.S. Department of Education.

Recruiting New Teachers. New releases: The urban teacher challenge. [Online]. *Recruiting New Teachers.* http://www.tnt.org/quick/press.html [2001, December 3].

Rodriguez, R. (1996). President's Hispanic Education Commission issue, long-awaited report. *Black Issues in Higher Education, 13*(16), 6–7.

Romo, H., and Falbo, T. (1996). *Latino high school graduation: Defying the odds.* Austin: University of Texas Press.

Ruiz, R. (1988). Orientations in language planning. In C. McKay and S. C. Wong (eds.), *Language diversity: Problem or resource* (pp. 3–25). Boston: Heinle and Heinle.

Ruiz, R. (1991). The empowerment of language minority students. In C. E. Sleeter (ed.), *Empowerment through multicultural education* (pp. 217–227). Albany, NY: State University of New York Press.

Rutstein, N. (1993). *Healing racism in America: A prescription for the disease.* Springfield, MA: Whitcomb Publishing.

Sharkey, C., and Layzer, J. (2000). Whose definition of success? *Tesol Quarterly, 34*(2), 352–374.

Skutnabb-Kangas, T. (1984). *Bilingualism or not: The education minorities.* Clevedon, England: Multilingual Matters.

Spradley, J. P. (1979). *The ethnographic interview.* New York: Holt, Rinehart and Winston.

Stavans, I. (1995). *The Hispanic condition: Reflections on culture and identity in America.* New York: Harper Collins.

Swisher, K. (1986). Authentic research: An interview on the way to Ponderosa. *Anthropology and Education Quarterly, 17*(2), 186–188.

Tangerine Unified School District. (1996–1997). *Secondary school-to-school profile.* Tucson, AZ: Author.

Tangerine Unified School District. (2000, November). *Affirmative action plan.* Tucson, AZ: Author.

Tapia, S. R. (1997, June 15). Public school alternative: Arizona leads nation in classroom experiments. *Arizona Daily Star*, p. 4a.

Unz, R. (2000, April/May). The right way for Republicans to handle ethnicity in politics. [Online]. *American Enterprise.* http://www.onenation.org/0004/0400.html [2001, June 6].

Valdes, G. (1996). *Con respeto: Bridging the distances between culturally diverse families and schools.* New York: Teachers College Press, Columbia University.

Valenzuela, A. (1999). *Substractive schooling: U.S. Mexican youth and the politics of caring.* Albany, NY: State University of New York Press.

van Zanten, A. (1997). Schooling immigrants in France in the 1990s: Success or failure of the republican model of integration? *Anthropology and Education Quarterly, 28*(3), 351–373.

Weis, L. (1985). *Between two worlds.* Boston: Routledge and Kegan Paul.

Wolcott, H. (1975). Criteria for an ethnographic approach to research in schools. *Human Organization, 34*(1), 111–128.

Zou, Y., and Trueba, E. (1998). *Ethnic identity and power: Cultural contexts of political action in school and society.* Albany: State University of New York Press.

INDEX

remedial programs in Arizona, 30, 81, 126, 132
Attrition rates. *See also* Dropout rates.
  of Latinos, 14
  of Latinos in Arizona, 29–32
Audio-visual support, 69
Availability of school services and programs, 129
Aztlan concept, 105

"Banking" transmission of knowledge, 126
Barrios, Latino segregation to, 23
Basic and remedial programs, 30, 81, 126, 132
Benevolent conspiracy, 18
Bicultural identity, 53
Bifocal identity, 52
Bilingual, stigma attached to term, 3
Bilingual education program, 8. *See also* English as a second language classes.
  absence of, and academic success, 19
  as anti-immigrant weapon, 8
  book shortage, 8
  in closed conservative educational community, 2
  "closeted" form of, 3
  as community-based pedagogy, 8
  coordinator, 80, 81
  depoliticizing, 8
  dismantling of, 6, 7, 10, 68, 126
  educators a discredit to the profession, 82
  educators, limited training of, 8
  as enriched instruction open to gifted and talented students, 84
  Latino's limited knowledge of, 20
  outlawing by Arizona and California, 6
  placing students on lower levels of society, 113
  psycho-educational benefits, 8
  reduced number of Latino students served in Arizona, 30
  remedial classes, 126
  student–teacher interactions, 82
  teacher shortage, 98–99
  teacher training funding and recruitment lacking, 30
  transitional quick-exit nature, 30
Bilingualism, 1
  importance explicated in national essay contest, 5
  as liability, 33

overt or covert negative messages to minority students, 5
  as punishable offense in 1960s school environment, 42
Blaming the victim, 9, 112
  for school failures, viii, 114, 133, 141
Border patrol agents, 23
Bordieu, P., 118, 120
Bureaucratic procedures, of high school, 43
Bush, George W., 6, 8, 28–29

California
  Latino population, 6, 23
  Proposition 227, 8
Call for service, of teachers in Mexico, 77
Care, in structural and historical perspective, xii, 57–58
Caring teachers, 57–58
Case study
  insider approach, 39
  Issues in Latino Education, 38–39
  Mountain High School, with case study student, Carla, 67–93, 137–147
  Presidio High School, with case study student, Manny, 41–65, 137–147
Annie E. Casey Foundation, 23–24
Certification of teachers, 9
Change agents, teachers as, 4
Charter schools, in Arizona, 30–31, 32
Chicano, connotation of term, 39
Chicano border tongues, 49
Chicano English (Spanglish), 49, 119, 120
Chicanos, 86
Chicanos por la Causa, 29
Choices, availability of, 110–111
Cholos, 86
Cinco de Mayo celebration, 88, 127
Classes, unavailability of, 127
Class organization, 75
Classroom environment, 51
Classroom experiments, in Arizona, 30
Classroom instruction, 125–128
Clinton, Hillary, 7
Closeness concept, of Latino families, 43
Clothing, bans on particular types of, 123
Collaborative communities of learning, 139
Collaborative cooperation within classroom, 124
Collaborative projects, among students of all races, 104
Collective worth, sense of, 119